Integrating the
PERFORMING ARTS

ARTS

in Grades K–5

Integrating the
PERFORMING
ARTS

in Grades K–5

Rekha S. Rajan

CORWIN
A SAGE Company

CORWIN
A SAGE Company

FOR INFORMATION:

Corwin
A SAGE Company
2455 Teller Road
Thousand Oaks, California 91320
(800) 233-9936
www.corwin.com

SAGE Publications Ltd.
1 Oliver's Yard
55 City Road
London EC1Y 1SP
United Kingdom

SAGE Publications India Pvt. Ltd.
B 1/I 1 Mohan Cooperative Industrial Area
Mathura Road, New Delhi 110 044
India

SAGE Publications Asia-Pacific Pte. Ltd.
3 Church Street
#10-04 Samsung Hub
Singapore 049483

Printed in the United States of America

A catalog record of this book is available from the Library of Congress.

ISBN 978-1-4522-0395-9

Acquisitions Editor: Jessica Allan
Associate Editor: Allison Scott
Editorial Assistant: Lisa Whitney
Production Editor: Amy Schroller
Copy Editor: Cate Huisman
Typesetter: C&M Digitals (P) Ltd.
Proofreader: Victoria Reed-Castro
Indexer: Judy Hunt
Cover Designer: Edgar Abarca
Permissions Editor: Karen Ehrmann

This book is printed on acid-free paper.

SUSTAINABLE FORESTRY INITIATIVE
Certified Chain of Custody
Promoting Sustainable Forestry
www.sfiprogram.org
SFI-01268
SFI label applies to text stock

12 13 14 15 16 10 9 8 7 6 5 4 3 2 1

Contents

PART III BEHIND THE CURTAIN

Acknowledgments

The concept of this book has been formulating in my mind for quite some time. As I have observed the value of the performing arts in children's lives, I have also been troubled with its absence in our schools.

The ideas in this book were generated from my experiences as a performer and teacher. I want to thank all of the children for whom I have had the pleasure of teaching music, theater, dance, and musical theater. There is no greater joy than seeing the vehicle for self-expression, confidence, and creativity that the performing arts provide. I am also grateful to the teachers and graduate and undergraduate students whose ideas have continued to inspire me in many ways.

Working with everyone at Corwin, particularly Jessica Allan, has been a wonderful experience. Jessica, your thoughtful, generous ideas have greatly helped shape this manuscript to what it is today. I knew from our first correspondence that you believed in the performing arts as much as I do, and I look forward to continuing our conversations on this topic.

My family is, of course, my greatest support system. I am always grateful to my in-laws for their support and prayers from afar! My brother and sister-in-law are eternal optimists, cheering on my every endeavor. To my parents, without whom none of this would be possible—you are both my best audience members. Thanks for always being in the front row. To my dad, for always driving me to auditions. To my mom, my first teacher, for showing me passion as an early childhood educator.

To my husband, Bharat, you are the most incredible person I have ever known. You constantly inspire me to be a better person with your dedication, kindness, and unconditional love. Although it has not been easy balancing our professional responsibilities with sleepless nights of changing diapers (now doubled!) I can always count on you to be there when I need you most.

To my son, Jagan, your smile motivates me, your hugs comfort me, and your laugh is my favorite music. To my daughter, Madhavi, you are everything beautiful in this world. This is for you both.

Publisher's Acknowledgments

Corwin gratefully acknowledges the contributions of the following reviewers:

Michelle Barnea, RN, MSEd
Early Childhood Educational Consultant
Innovations in Early Learning
Millburn, NJ

Karla Bronzynski
First Grade Teacher
Eldora–New Providence Schools/Iowa Reading Association
Eldora, IA

Rebecca S. Compton
Professor, Elementary Education
East Central University
College of Education
Ada, OK

Tamara Daugherty
Third Grade Teacher
Lakeville Elementary School
Apopka, FL

Stacey B. Ferguson, NBCT
Teacher Consultant, Live Oak Writing Project
Bay Saint Louis, MS

Kimberly Kyff, NBCT
Literacy Coach
Detroit Public Schools
Detroit, MI

About the Author

Rekha S. Rajan, EdD is an arts education specialist with a focus on early childhood education and assessment. She holds a doctorate in music education from Teachers College, Columbia University, where she also received an EdM in music education. She also holds an MA in early childhood professions from Roosevelt University.

Dr. Rajan is a senior research associate with the Center for Arts Education Research at Teachers College, Columbia University, where she is part of ArtsResearch, a team of consultants who evaluate arts-based partnerships around the United States. Through these partnerships, she has interviewed and observed hundreds of public school teachers regarding the strengths and challenges they face with integrating the arts.

Her research interests focus on the impact of the performing arts in the lives of young children and on teachers' use of the performing arts in the classroom. She has published articles in *General Music Today*, *Focus on Pre-K&K* and *Focus on Elementary* of the *Association of Childhood Education International,* and is also the author of the forthcoming book, *Children's Experiences in Musical Theater.*

Dr. Rajan has held faculty positions at National-Louis University, where she coordinated the graduate programs in early childhood education, and Roosevelt University where she taught courses in elementary education and supervised student teachers. She has been working with teachers and teacher candidates for more than 10 years, and sits on various Illinois state councils and advisory committees for early childhood assessment. Dr. Rajan is also the president and founder of the Greater Chicago Area Chapter of the Early Childhood Music and Movement Association. Prior to teaching in higher education, Dr. Rajan taught music, theater, and dance in studio and classroom settings, and performed in numerous operas, operettas, and musicals.

PART I

From Practice to Performance

1

An Introduction to the Performing Arts

A young child sits at the piano for the first time, running his hands across the keys, kicking his legs beneath him as they dangle off the bench.

As the curtain rises, a family sits together in the center aisle to watch the opening night performance of a new play.

Two sisters dance together in their bedroom, creating their own choreography to their favorite music, twirling and swirling to the sounds around them.

A cast of children stand anxious and excited on stage in the bright spotlights, adorned in colorful costumes.

These vignettes are examples of music, theater, dance, and musical theater—artistic genres that are individually and collectively defined as the performing arts.

The performing arts are a vital and necessary part of our culture and society and exist in many formal and informal settings. Live performances in large arenas, our favorite songs and recordings, television shows, community theater productions, and informal dance halls all provide venues for experiencing music, theater, dance, and musical theater. We cherish the opportunity to watch our favorite play or musical, sing our favorite songs, or dance to our favorite music. The performing arts are an important part of our lives, our communication, and our self-expression. These arts forms are categorized as such because of how each embodies the idea of practice to performance: the process of experiencing, studying, watching, or performing a piece of music, script, or choreography.

When you think of *performance,* what comes to mind? Is it a soundstage with your favorite performer, a dance club, an elementary school production? Performance is simply defined as *an event that involves a group of people,* but this is not always equated to a live performance, in front of an audience of thousands of individuals. A performance can be personal and intimate or social and culturally influenced. While the performing arts are traditionally relegated to intense years of formal study and practice, recent years have shown a resurgence of interest in younger participants who are acting, singing, and dancing in various venues.

Popular culture has played a large part in this interest in the performing arts for all individuals regardless of background knowledge, training, and talent, as the most predominant societal view is one that encourages the idea that *anyone* can sing, act, and dance. Reality shows, audition opportunities, and community performances invite universal participation. Interestingly, recent trends have also documented a resurgence of participation from school-aged children within school, community, and professional musical theater (Rajan, in press).

While the performing arts in our communities are thriving with participation and performances, these arts forms are notably absent in our schools. If the performing arts are an important component of our lives and learning, how come they are not a stronger part of the educational curriculum and core? The answer is simply what most teachers recognize on a daily basis—a strong push for accountability and testing, which has substantially diminished the arts in our schools. The further absence of teaching artists and arts specialists in schools often places the responsibility on classroom teachers to find creative ways to integrate the arts, to foster artistic experiences in the classroom that will positively impact learning.

This common solution is an unfair and unrealistic expectation to add to the already high demands that classroom teachers face. Furthermore, teachers are not always confident with teaching the arts, and a multitude of challenges exist with arts integration such as securing resources, props, and supplies for these various experiences. Even if the performing arts belong in our schools, the questions frequently asked by educators and administrators are *why should we teach the arts*, and *what are students learning?*

It is an expectation in the field of early childhood and elementary education today that children in preprimary settings are already learning in an environment that is heavily focused on exploration, hands-on learning, and artistic experiences. More so, it is in the elementary classroom that children further need creative venues that encourage self-confidence, self-expression, and collaboration—personal and social skills that are an integral component of learning and development.

For many years, children have commonly studied music or dance in private studio settings, pursuing these art forms as extracurricular activities. Much of the current research on artistic learning focuses on integrated, in-school experiences, where the term *dance* is often used synonymously with movement, and the term *theater* is used synonymously with drama activities. Regardless of name, research has documented how children gain not only artistic skills, but improve academically, personally, and socially through the arts (Burton, Horowitz, & Abeles, 2000; Horowitz & Rajan, 2007; Rajan, 2009, 2011; Upitis & Smithrim, 2003).

Integrated arts are simply defined as the connection between one or more academic subjects (such as math, science, social studies, and language arts) and one or more performing arts form (music, theater, dance, and musical theater). Through observations, interviews, and students' reflections on and perceptions of their experiences, educators have documented how children's participation as singers, actors, and dancers positively impacts their learning. Some findings include demonstrated growth in self-confidence and self-expression, new friendships with peers, and augmented connections between arts learning and academic subject matter (Burton, et al., 2000; Feay-Shaw, 2001; Rajan, 2009; Roberts, 2007).

This book addresses the various needs and challenges teachers face today and provides a resource of research-based, practical ideas for integrating music, theater, dance, and musical theater into grades K–5. The book is organized into three sections building on the definitions of the performing arts as artistic genres and disciplines of study as presented in this introduction.

The first section, Chapters 1 and 2, provides an overview of the book and some general theories and practices for the integration of the performing arts into classroom activities.

The second section provides detailed portraits of each of the performing arts forms presented through descriptions drawn from research and literature, examples from the classroom and community, and complete lesson plans for integrating the performing arts into math, science, social studies, and language arts. The lesson plans include specific suggestions with learning objectives and appropriate methods for assessing learning in the performing arts and related content areas. While there are often specific suggestions or topics for music, theater, dance, and musical theater excerpts provided within lessons, these topics can easily be modified to best suit your own curricular needs.

In order to provide a wide range of ideas for each subject area and maintain brevity in the text, each chapter in this section includes 16 lesson plans. While each grade level is not necessarily represented, the range in topics and flexibility in the lessons is intended as a springboard for your own teaching contexts, a vehicle from which you will build your own activities fused with the performing arts.

Cognitive skills and brain-based learning are also of great importance to educators and often provide a means of justifying the arts in the classroom. For this reason, each chapter has a table that outlines the personal, social, and artistic skills that are developed through the integrated performing arts lessons. Each chapter also includes a description of the process of planning arts-integrated lessons and a section entitled Building Artistic Vocabulary that highlights key terms in each of the artistic genres. Finally, this section includes opportunities for reflecting on the meaning of the performing arts in our own lives as audience members, active participants, students, and teachers.

It was most important to ensure that relevant standards were also addressed and discussed for each performing arts form. Although each state has specific early learning standards that are required for developing and implementing lessons, throughout this book you will find reference to the Early Childhood Standards for teachers in K–3 settings, developed by the National Association for the Education of Young Children (NAEYC); the Elementary Standards for teachers in grades 4–5, developed by the Association of Childhood Education International (ACEI); and the Common Core State Standards for Math and Language Arts (CC).

The National Standards for Arts Education (music, theater, and dance) were developed in 1994 as a product of the Consortium of National Arts Education Association. The standards are found and housed within the individual arts organizations—The National Association for Music Education (NAFME), the American Alliance for Theatre and Education (AATE), and the National Dance Education Organization (NDEO).

Individually, these standards represent the requirements and benchmarks deemed most important for the arts and children's education in each respective field. Collectively, they present a comprehensive approach to integrating the performing arts in a way that maintains the integrity of the arts and addresses the needs and challenges of educators in various settings.

Please note that while the appropriate standards are noted at the beginning of each lesson, the list of referenced standards can be found in the appendix of this book. For a *complete* list of all the standards, please contact or refer to the appropriate organization—correlating websites and links are also included in the appendix.

The third and final section of this book delves deeper into building and sustaining integrated performing arts experiences within the school, community, and professional settings. Finally, I challenge each of you to become artistically reflective educators, in that you continue to recognize your own artistic experiences (both good and bad!) to shape the performing arts experiences that you will create and implement with your students, within your classrooms. With these various resources and references, it is my hope that the performing arts will find a relevant and meaningful place in your own curriculum and teaching contexts.

2

The Classroom Stage

In the world's audience hall, the simple blade of grass sits on the
same carpet with the sunbeams, and the stars of midnight

—Rabindranath Tagore

Imagine your ideal classroom. What would it consist of? How would the desks, chairs, shelves, and rugs be arranged? How would the classroom flow? What materials, manipulatives, activities, or centers would you have for your students? What is nonnegotiable?

A Performance Space

A classroom centered on the performing arts should have a stage, a performance space for students to explore their ideas, express themselves, and collaborate with peers in formal and improvised performances.

Clearly, this is not always a realistic or attainable goal. Many classrooms are simply too small to dedicate any location for a stage, and some teachers and schools do not have the resources or funds to develop such a venue within the classroom. The foundation for this book is the idea that students *should* have a place to perform, that the space within which students explore the performing arts is as important as the performing arts themselves. In fact, for many students, it is the act of performing—the final product of the rehearsals and practices—that is the most important part (Lazaroff, 2001).

Performance spaces range in setting, style, and location. Some spaces are simply a result of convenience, while others are the result of a specific goal or purpose. Consider the venues where you have observed an individual acting, singing, or dancing—in large performance halls, on the sidewalks of a busy city, by the pillars of the subway platforms, in religious venues, coffee shops, auditoriums, gymnasiums, basements, and cafeterias. Where does the classroom fit into this list?

Consider the arrangement of your own classroom. (If you do not have your own classroom, observe the classroom of any teacher, peer, or mentor as a starting point.) Is there any opportunity for students to move freely or find their own space when engaging in an activity? How are the desks arranged? How are students seated—in rows? Small groups? You may find that the more open classrooms are those for the younger students, and as the grades increase, so too do the limitations of the classroom space. Much of this is due to the focus on teaching and learning different skills, content, and subjects with older students and a greater emphasis in upper elementary grades on individual instruction rather than group work and collaboration.

If your school setting has access to a gymnasium or any classrooms that are open and not used (some schools have dance studios or even small auditoriums), these are ideal spaces that are ready to use and require minimal preparation time.

It is important to note that a performance space does not have to be a stage in the traditional sense—a centered, rectangular platform; rather, consider the idea of designating a space just for performances. Rearranging desks and tables to create a performance space in the center of the classroom, or an open corner where audience members can be seated in rows, would serve the function well.

Many successful performances by elementary students have also been presented in school cafeterias, basements that are open and have windows (so as not to feel too enclosed), and even outdoors (weather permitting), where students can experience watching an outdoor concert or play.

Some of the benefits of limiting the space for performances are also the limits on the resources needed to present such a production. The larger the venue, the greater the need for a sound system, microphones, lighting, and other technical supports for a performance that are not always readily available to teachers. If the classroom is the stage, the feeling is more intimate—families and friends are provided the opportunity to see students perform up close and experience the classroom in a new dimension. Rehearsals are also easier in this process, as students do not have to take the actions and choreography they rehearsed in the classroom and translate them to fit into a different performance space.

As you plan for a performance space, ask your students what they believe would make an ideal stage. Perhaps they want to construct a stage for performances (see the activity *Shaping the Stage* in Chapter 4 for a related lesson idea), or have strong ideas of where they would want to perform. Inviting students' participation in this decision gives them ownership over their performances, making it a classroom vision rather than one individual's decision.

Most important, by designating a performance space within the classroom, the performing arts become a part of the learning environment, rather than something different and separated, giving this experience as much value and importance as other academic subjects.

Audience and Ambience

What does it mean to be a good audience? What are some qualities and characteristics that come to mind? Ask musicians, actors, or dancers how they define the role of the audience during a show, and they will most likely state that *without the audience, there is no performance.*

The audience is as important as the actual performance (if not more so). Consider how the success of a new Broadway musical, the fame of a rock star, or the appeal of a comedic actor is all contingent upon the audience response to the performance. Many careers, performances, and productions have failed simply due to negative audience response or a lack of audience support. Similarly, there are award ceremonies and celebrations (e.g., the Billboard Music Awards) that recognize an artist's appeal and success based solely on audience reaction.

Many studies have focused on the audience perspective—the impact of watching a live performance and of participating in a show as an audience member—and the learning that takes place during this time. Stephanie Pitts (2005) documented how the audience members in various music festivals enjoyed being able to participate and interact with performers and how they developed a sense of community while watching a live performance. Matthew Reason (2010) explored how children watch live theater performances; their attitudes, perceptions, and perspectives with being in the audience; and the impact of these experiences on their learning about various theatrical shows and societal messages.

Teaching your students through integrated performing arts activities allows them to experience the process of creating art, the dimensions of being on stage, and a chance to take ownership over their ideas and collaborate with peers. Additionally, teaching your students how to be good audience members reinforces the concepts of patience, acceptance, respecting one another, and being supportive and encouraging.

Teachers often use the start of the school year to set ground rules and establish boundaries and expectations for the classroom. This is a great time to create a list of the criteria that constitute being a good audience. Invite students to share their own perspectives, to contribute to this list, to define *audience* in their own words. Ask students if they have ever been an audience member in a live show, in a movie theater, at a school performance. How did the audience act? Where were people sitting? What did the space look like? Where would the audience be seated in their classroom performances?

Here are some of the common factors of audience etiquette, intended to serve as starting points for these discussions:

- Be respectful and patient.
- Be focused.
- Observe the performance.
- Do not talk loudly (or use cell phones or send text messages!).
- Do not enter after a performance has started.
- Do not get up and leave before a performance ends.
- Relax and enjoy the show.
- Give applause and encores for the performers.

While these criteria are the "standard" protocol for being a good audience member, many performances actually invite audience participation; they encourage talking and sharing of ideas, or contributions to the plot and development of the show. Discussing these variations is also important, so students realize that it is not a punishment to be in the audience; rather, it is a central, vital role to the success of a show.

Many educators and artists unequivocally contend that classroom discussions simply don't compare with the experience of actually being in the audience of a professional show. The individual perceptions; the shared sense of community and enjoyment; and the artistic ambience of the dimmed lights, raised curtains, and surrounding music are, on some levels, unexplainable. For students to truly understand the role of the audience, they need to actually experience this firsthand.

A novel idea for defining the role of an audience member is to have students track their own reflections and perspectives in a journal, through artwork, or through group discussions after a performance. Pose some guiding questions: What was it like being in the audience? What did they enjoy? What was challenging? If they were the performers, what expectations would they have for the audience?

Before integrating the performing arts into your classroom (or if you have done so already, as a means of expanding these horizons), take your students outside of the school environment, into the performance venues, spaces, and halls where music, theater, dance, and musical theater resonate. These experiences, when translated into the classroom, will have context and meaning beyond just words and ideas.

PART II

Integrating the Performing Arts

3

An Introduction
to Music

Music, if it be in reality an expressive language, suggests every-
thing to children if they are left to themselves.

—Maria Montessori

Madi is kicking her legs beneath her as she pushes back and forth on the playground swing. She is humming to herself and suddenly bursts out in song—*It's beautiful today, the sun is on my face!*
It's beautiful today, the sun is on my feet.

Her mother, seated on a swing next to her asks, *where did you hear that song, Madi?*

It's mine. Madi replies. *It's a song about how I feel.*

The Melodies of Childhood

Music is a natural part of childhood. Familiar songs, invented lyrics, spontaneous rhythms, and recognizable beats are all examples of how children naturally engage in musical behaviors. Through music making, children are engaged with their senses: They listen to the complex sounds around them, move their bodies to the rhythms, and touch and feel the textures and shapes of instruments.

In any authentic setting (a context beyond the school doors), take a moment and observe the children around you. What you might notice is rhythmic footsteps, humming and singing, patterned hand games, chanting and dancing. Consider whether these behaviors had a catalyst—is the child alone? Engaging in play or conversation with another child, an adult? Where did these spontaneous musical behaviors come from?

In one of the most prominent sources in the literature on children's music making, Patricia Shehan Campbell (1998) explores how children express themselves through music, communicate with one another, and find meaning in their own lives. Not only do children make music, but music is an inevitable part of their lives, affording them an alternative way to communicate, to be inventive, and to be creative.

Similarly, in her in-depth, culturally sensitive account of children's musical play, Kathryn Marsh (2008) illustrates the importance of music in children's lives through the melodies that they create, which eventually shape and define their childhoods. Importantly, these experiences and activities are child initiated, brought forth through the social factors present in a given context, and channeled through children's natural inclination toward being musical.

What does this mean for music in our elementary schools? It is commonly known (though not always spoken of) that music programs are often the first to be eliminated when budget cuts make their dreaded appearances. Parents, teachers, and administrators alike will proudly share examples of children's musical behaviors—or reflect on the impact music has made in their own lives—yet this contradicts the challenged, often troubled role music has within our schools. Arts educators have long engaged in debates on the role of the arts in our schools and have battled between integrating the arts into the curriculum, on the one hand, and, on the other, placing arts as a part of the curriculum for art's sake and none other (Davis, 2007; Jensen, 2001).

Music has a primary stance in the preschool classroom, where children are greeted with morning songs and listen to music as they transition from one activity to the next. Unfortunately, music has a minimal role in elementary school, where the emphasis is on demonstrating academic achievement through standardized tests. In the absence of a music specialist, resourceful teachers often take it upon themselves to integrate music into the curriculum.

Musical activities are often tied to language arts to encourage creativity, stimulate imagination, or enhance student achievement. Children's literature can be connected to various disciplines, and "within the music curriculum it can encourage creativity, reinforce music skills and knowledge, enhance listening, and expand multicultural awareness" (Fallin, 1995, p. 24). Combining reading children's books with a musical activity supports cooperative learning experiences through peer groups and discussions (Fisher & McDonald, 2001).

Group musical activities often motivate elementary students to participate and engage in daily classroom activities. Group music activities in the classroom can establish a safe, social environment and may also enhance a student's interest in a subject. When students are presented with group music activities at the beginning of class, there is a greater likelihood that they will independently choose to engage in those same activities at a later time (Turner, 1999). When children are given the freedom to choose activities that they want to participate in, they become more intrinsically motivated to engage in musical or artistic endeavors.

While the music classroom fosters opportunities for individual vocal development, the general classroom environment traditionally promotes group singing experiences. Children in elementary school often participate in singing activities that focus on skill development, pitch, and accuracy (Hale, 2006). Singing is an important part of children's lives as they express themselves and interact with their environment through spontaneous vocalizations (Chooi-Theng Lew & Campbell, 2005). Although in-school musical experiences have transformed to include a variety of activities, singing continues to be one of the primary components of the elementary music curriculum (Mizener, 1990).

Through music (both self-initiated and teacher instructed), children build confidence in themselves, augment their self-esteem, improve focus and memorization, and demonstrate motivation to participate in activities. Children also learn to work cooperatively, collaborate with peers, take turns, and share instruments. In their own words, children have also described how they have become better singers and songwriters, how they express themselves through song, and how they feel happy when they sing (Hale, 2006; Rajan, 2009).

The personal, social, and musical skills that are fostered through integrated music activities are summarized in Table 3.1 and serve as a foundation for the examples, vignettes, and lessons presented within this chapter.

| Table 3.1 | Learning Through Integrated Activities in Music |

Personal Learning	Self-Confidence, Self-Esteem, Focus, Motivation, Memorization
Social Learning	Cooperation, Collaboration, Taking Turns, Sharing
Musical Learning	Self-Expression, Vocal Skills, Musical Skills, Understanding of Rhythm, Beats, Patterns, Timbre, and Texture

Integrating Music

The ideas and suggestions for integrating music into grades K–5 presented here are meant to be starting points for lessons and activities that have the most meaning within your own teaching context and curriculum. Some of the activities presented here are specific in their focus and connection to various subject areas, while others are broad and general, aimed at re-energizing your teaching and learning experience with your students.

Musical Autobiography

Reflect on the role of music in your life—the impact music has made in shaping your decisions and providing references for important places and times, and the associations you have with particular songs or musical pieces. Use the following prompts to guide your self-reflections:

- My favorite experience with music is . . .
- My earliest memory with music is . . .
- My greatest challenge with music is . . .
- My favorite song is . . . because . . .
- My comfort level with music is . . . because . . .

From these starting points, consider whether you have ever integrated music (in any form) into your classroom. If your answer is yes, why did you choose to do so? Was it music playing in the background? A greeting song that everyone sings? If your answer is no, why not? Were you hesitant to integrate this art form? Uncomfortable with singing alone?

Recognizing your own experiences, comfort level, strengths, and challenges with music will strengthen how you integrate music into the curriculum. Consider the types of music you listen to and the range of genres that comprise your personal repertoire, and begin to identify ways of drawing in students' musical preferences to encourage participation and involvement in the classroom.

The Process of Integrating Music

Many teachers use music in a variety of ways in their classroom. Some examples include playing familiar songs for students to listen to, using background music while students complete specific tasks, or group singing and instrument playing. Music in the elementary classroom does not need to be limited to these basic uses; rather, it should be integrated seamlessly into existing lessons and activities. Music can be used to teach students about different cultures and provide them with opportunities for creating and improvising tunes, interpreting and analyzing music from various parts of the world, and exploring instrument sounds, textures, and timbres.

To broaden your use of music in the classroom, begin with the National Standards for Music Education (NAFME, 1994) and the standards specific to your grade level (grouped as K–4 and 5–8 in these standards). Some of the basic elements of music include singing, listening, playing, making, improvising, composing, and evaluating music, as well as understanding the relationship between music and other disciplines and identifying music of various cultures and contexts.

When building a lesson with music integrated into it, focus initially on the specific learning objectives within the lesson. For example, kindergartners learning about weather can contribute ideas for a class song on weather; third-grade students can compare the musical styles of Indian, Chinese, and Japanese music; or fifth-grade students can interpret a folk song to understand how time and place impact culture.

As you create lessons, talk about, and use music in your classroom, consider ways of introducing or reinforcing the following musical terminology. These are basic terms and definitions that will serve as a foundation for creating and discussing music.

Building Artistic Vocabulary

Beat: Music's steady pulse

Dynamics: The volume of sounds

Harmony: The blending of sounds; this may be produced by two or more sounds performed at the same time

Improvisation: The process of creating music in the moment (prominent in early Western classical, South Indian classical, and jazz music)

Melody: The tune of music; the pattern of sounds that make up the musical composition

Pitch: The highs and lows of musical sound patterns

Rhythm: The pattern and beat of music

Tempo: The speed at which a piece of music is played or sung

Timbre: The tone of sound; for example, the uniquely differently qualities produced by a steel drum or a bongo drum

Vignettes and Viewpoints

The ways in which children learn and interact through music in authentic and instruction-based settings are varied and unique. After reading through each vignette, consider your own viewpoint with the following questions:

- Is there a catalyst for the musical behavior?
- Can this scenario/activity be integrated into my own teaching context?
- What would my students learn from this experience?
- How would I assess students' personal, social, and musical learning?

Two boys are running in the park, chasing one another in circles. One boy pauses and picks up a stick from the ground. He holds it to his mouth and pretends to play a trumpet. He makes tooting sounds as if he is blowing a horn. The other boy finds two more sticks and sits on the grass. He begins beating the sticks in rhythmic succession and chants—boom boom ch, boom boom ch.

Mr. J introduces the second graders in his class to the bongo drum, a percussion instrument from Cuba. He asks the students if anyone has ever seen this instrument before. One girl nods, stating that she has seen those drums played on TV. Mr. J demonstrates a short pattern of drumming for the students and asks the class if anyone wants to take a turn. Several students animatedly raise their hands. Mr. J calls upon the same girl who recognized the instrument. She skips up to the bongo and hits it with both hands at the same time, then slows down, alternating her hands in a steady beat.

A young girl is riding in the car and listening to the music on the radio. She hears a familiar song and starts singing out loud. She is bopping her head to the beat and shaking her hands in simple dance moves. After the song ends, she continues singing, bopping her head, and shaking her hands.

The fifth graders in Ms. M's class are listening to a traditional American folk song. Students are instructed to listen to the lyrics, consider the tune of the melody, and consider the instruments used in the music. Ms. M asks students to analyze the music, describing how the melody relates to the lyrics. One student remarks that the music sounds sad and lonely and that the flute in the background sounds as though the singer is wishing for someone far away.

Music Activities for Motivation and Movement

Music is clearly a part of children's lives—their personal time and social interactions. In this section, I have presented three popular music activities that are used by teachers and professional artists within school and community settings.

Each activity has been modified so that it is appropriate for students in elementary school. The explanation includes specific skills that are being reinforced. Importantly, each of these activities fosters personal learning (focus, clarity of thought, self-expression) and social learning (large groups, awareness of space) through music. Your students will enjoy the opportunity to relax, re-energize, and just listen to the music.

My Music, My Space

Take a moment with your students to breathe in deeply, relax your body, and clear your mind. Ask students to find their own space in the classroom—either standing, seated, or lying down. Play music in the background and ask students to clear their minds, focus only on their breathing.

Skills—This activity will focus and relax your students (ideal for mornings or midafternoons). A variety of music can be used—either instrumental or vocal. Begin by selecting a few of your own favorite songs and pieces, and then ask your students to bring in musical selections for this activity. Based on the time allotted during the day, you can structure this activity to be 30 seconds or 10 minutes long.

Free Dance, Freeze Dance

Encourage students to participate in a group free dance or freeze dance. Play lively, upbeat music, and provide students with the opportunity to move however and wherever they like in the classroom. You can modify the activity by making it a freeze dance (pausing the music at random intervals), or including specific movements at certain times (ones that may correlate with the music).

Skills—This activity is great for the kinesthetic leaner and will likely motivate your students, releasing their giggles and tensions and allowing them time to let loose in the classroom. Consider using popular songs that your students will recognize, as they will be more likely to participate and dance!

Oodles of Doodles

Provide students with blank paper and pencils, pens, crayons, or markers. As you play a song or piece of instrumental music, encourage them to draw, scribble, write, or doodle whatever comes to mind. Provide students with opportunities to share their work (if they choose) and to select music to play on another occasion.

Skills—Students will cherish the opportunity to doodle in class and to express their thoughts and feelings freely as they listen to the music. Some students may take this activity more seriously than others, presenting products that are representative of their thoughts, concerns, or fears. The activity may be particularly useful to visual learners. Remember that students do not have to share work, but they should be encouraged to do so if they seem inclined to present their doodles. This activity could also be connected to another lesson or subject area being taught—perhaps for students who are having trouble staying on task and need redirecting, or for those who finished their work very quickly.

Lessons and Assessments

Music, a ubiquitous part of our lives and communities, can be easily connected to math, science, social studies, and language arts activities. In this section you will find 16 lessons focused on integrating music into math, science, social studies, and language arts through singing, listening, playing instruments, making instruments, and moving. Each lesson, while specific in nature and content, can be easily modified, or a different song, piece of music, text, or subject can be substituted for the one described.

Also included are learning objectives; standards for music education, early childhood education, and elementary education; and the Common Core standards. There are also specific procedures for implementation of the lessons, extensions to the activity, and assessments. There are a variety of instruments that can be used to assess the arts (such as performance assessments, work samples, portfolios, and video and audio documentation), but to make these lessons practical and applicable to your teaching contexts, I include assessments that are focused on meeting the learning objectives, but they could be easily modified.

The arts standards presented for each lesson are taken from the National Standards for Music Education (NAFME, 1994) and are grouped by grades—one set of standards for grades K–4 and another for grades 5–8. Each lesson is also connected to the relevant core standards for early childhood (NAEYC) or elementary education (ACEI). These standards are upheld by educational professionals across the United States and promote active self-reflection and professional development in teachers. The addition of the early childhood and elementary education standards is in line with the goal of this book to continue and foster a cycle of self-reflection that is necessary for integrating the performing arts into your classroom.

It is impossible to add specific content area learning standards to any of these lessons, as such standards are specific to various regional requirements, but included you will find the Common Core standards for math and language arts. Therefore, when writing your own integrated lessons (or modifying these to fit your own curriculum), I strongly recommend incorporating content area standards to strengthen and build the connections made through these integrated activities.

Shape Hokey Pokey

Content Areas: Music, Math

Grade Level: Kindergarten

Learning Objectives

1. Students will identify the correct shape from four different options presented to them (e.g., square, triangle, circle, diamond).

2. Students will match the shape with the correct shape sung in the song. (See procedures for song lyrics.)

3. Students will actively participate, and sing the lyrics of the song.

Standards

- National Standards for Music Education K–4
  - Content Standard 1—Achievement Standards(a)(c)
- National Standards for Early Childhood Education
  - Standard 1(a)(c)
  - Standard 3(b)
- Common Core State Standards
  - K.G.2.

Procedures

Present students with four shapes that they are starting to learn about or have minimally familiarized themselves with. Each student should have cutouts of each of the four shapes. (The students can make their own cutouts from felt, poster board, or any other material.)

Gather students in a group and introduce a new song to them about shapes:

Shape Song (to the tune of Hokey Pokey)

You put the square shape in, you take the square shape out
You put the square shape in, and you shake it all about
Square, circle, or triangles, we're turning all around,
We're finding all our shapes out!

Have students sing through the song, repeating a line at a time to familiarize themselves with the lyrics and purpose. Demonstrate for the students that when each shape is named, they have to select the appropriate shape from their four choices.

Extensions

After singing through the song a few times and practicing with the shapes, allow students to take turns leading the song, selecting which shape should be called. The difficulty of the lesson can be increased by adding more shapes to the mix (such as eight instead of four) or adding more complex shapes.

Assessments

1. Have students complete the Shape Song Worksheet.

2. Students should be able to match at least 50% of the shapes to what is called out in the song during the first few times this activity is presented.

3. Observe students to note who is singing along and actively participating.

Shape Song Worksheet
Draw the shapes you sang in the song:

Rainy Day Rainstick

Content Areas: Music, Math, Visual Art

Grade Level: Second

Learning Objectives

1. Students will identify the qualities of the cylinder shape.

2. Students will describe the purpose of a rainstick.

3. Students will measure and create their own rainsticks for a class performance.

Standards

- National Standards for Music Education K–4
  - Content Standard 1—Achievement Standards(b)(c)
- National Standards for Early Childhood Education
  - Standard 1(a)
  - Standard 3(b)
- Common Core State Standards
  - 2.MD.1.

Procedures

Rainsticks have a unique history, as they are believed to be instruments that can change the weather. Their origination is debated. While some believe rainsticks were created and used in Latin America (Peru and Chile), others believe that they originated in West African folklore. Their purpose remains the same, regardless of geographic location: to bring rain to drought filled regions.

Explain to students that rainsticks were traditionally made from the cactus plant, where the plant dried out and the thorns were removed. The hollow, dried plant was then filled with pebbles or stones and turned in various patterns and directions to emulate the sound of falling rain. Today, rainsticks can be made with more simple materials (paper towel or toilet paper rolls) and are decorated with feathers and ribbons.

To make a rainstick, begin with an empty paper towel roll and cover one end with a small piece of cardboard or aluminum foil. The foil should be either taped to the roll or wrapped in place with a rubber band. Fill the roll with small rocks or pasta, and then seal the other end in a similar fashion. Decorate the stick with vibrant colors and images.

Engage students in a conversation about why rainsticks were important years ago and how they might still have relevance today. Do we need rainsticks today? Why or why not?

Have students carefully measure and identify the various characteristics of their own rainsticks. If they choose to make one with a paper towel roll, how are the dimensions and sounds different from one made from a smaller product, such as a toilet paper roll?

Ask students to perform a rain dance with their rainsticks. Invite students to create all the components of this dance so that they take ownership of their performance. What steps are a part of the dance? What is the story being told? How will the audience know we are asking for rain?

Extensions

Reading *The Rainstick: A Fable*, by Sandra Chisholm Robinson (TwoDot, 1994), is a nice introduction to this lesson, or it can be an extension activity for students to read at home. Students can also create their own stories for the rainstick (creative writing) or invent another instrument that has a specific, weather related purpose (science).

Assessments

1. Students should be able to make simple measurements and verbally (or in writing) describe the various characteristics of the cylinder shape, including basic dimensions and perimeter.

2. Ask students to write a short journal entry (one paragraph minimum) that describes why rainsticks were important, who used rainsticks, and the relevance of rainsticks today.

3. Each student should have created a rainstick as a final product for the performance.

Don't Be So Blue Danube

Content Areas: Music, Math, Language Arts

Grade Level: Fourth

Learning Objectives

1. Students will identify the patterns in the piece The Blue Danube, by Johann Strauss, Jr.

2. Students will describe the correlation between the music and the composer's title.

3. Students will interpret the characteristics of a waltz through creative writing and artwork.

Standards

- National Standards for Music Education K–4
  - Content Standard 6—Achievement Standards(b)(c)
  - Content Standard 9—Achievement Standards(a)(b)
- National Standards for Elementary Education
  - Standard 2(2.3)(2.5)
  - Standard 3(3.1)
- Common Core State Standards
  - OA.5.

Procedures

The Blue Danube is perhaps the most famous waltz in classical music history. Composed by the Austrian composer, Johann Strauss, Jr., in 1866, the tune has been associated with everything from ballroom dances in high society to animated shorts in popular culture. The title refers to Europe's second longest river (the Danube) and is translated from the original German title of On the Beautiful, Blue Danube. The piece was originally an instrumental orchestration, but lyrics were later written and added to vocal performances.

Play a selection of the waltz (performed on any orchestral recording), and ask students to listen to the patterns that they hear. Specifically, the waltz is recognized for the steady, three-beat pattern that can be counted throughout the music. It is important to play the music several times to ensure that students can feel and recognize the steady beat. Ask open-ended questions, such as, "What other patterns do they hear in the instruments? What is the symbolism of the three-beat pattern?"

As students continue to listen to the music, ask them to interpret the sounds and patterns by posing questions about the imagery that it evokes—a setting, time, or place. Are there people? What are they doing? What could the composer have intended with this music?

Extensions

A light-hearted extension to this lesson is to play the animated clip entitled *The Blue Danube,* made in 1939 from MGM. Challenge students to analyze and interpret the music in relation to the animation. Is the waltz an appropriate selection? What other musical excerpt or pattern would work? What animation would be more appropriate? While this clip may be challenging to locate, it is currently available on several Internet video sites or through various MGM "released to DVD" compilations.

Additionally, The Blue Danube is played in several sections of Stanley Kubrick's *2001: A Space Odyssey, The Adventures of Rocky and Bullwinkle,* and even *Austin Powers.*

Importantly, the purpose of this lesson is to have students analyze and interpret the strong mathematical patterns that compose Western classical music, and their relevance in popular culture today. Any classical piece can be substituted in this lesson, but compositions by Wolfgang Amadeus Mozart, or pieces such as The Blue Danube and other waltzes, have the strongest, most repetitive, and most easily distinguishable patterns.

Assessments

1. Students individually recognize not only the three-part pattern in the waltz but also other rhythmic patterns in excerpts from other musical pieces.

2. Students should be able to describe the relationship between the music and the composer's title—what the relationship is and how the three-part pattern reflects the title.

3. Each student should complete a short journal entry accompanied by a work of art that presents her or his own interpretation of the music, setting, and location, and an alternate title for the orchestration.

The Wind Is in My Hair

Content Areas: Music, Science

Grade Level: Kindergarten

Learning Objectives

1. Students will identify the characteristics of four types of weather.

2. Students will provide suggestions for how the weather will impact their bodies when outside.

3. Students will participate in the creation and performance of a group song.

Standards

- National Standards for Music Education K–4
  - o Content Standard 1—Achievement Standard(c)
  - o Content Standard 4—Achievement Standard(a)
- National Standards for Early Childhood Education
  - o Standard 1(b)
  - o Standard 3(b)
  - o Standard 4(b)

Procedures

Begin the class by asking students to list different weather conditions. (These can either be the basis for the song in this lesson or for a larger discussion, if you have already decided what four elements to focus on.) Once the four different weather conditions have been decided, talk to the students about the characteristics of the weather. Ask questions such as, What happens to your body? How does your face feel? What happens to your hair? Can you feel the weather on your hands or nose?

To the tune of "Farmer in the Dell," ask students to help you create new lyrics to the music. For example,

> The wind can blow my hair, the wind can blow my hair
> When I am outside, the wind can blow my hair.

Some other examples include rain drops on my nose, snow falls on my hands, sun shines on my face, hail taps on my toes, sun will make me sweat, the rain puddles are wet, and snowflakes on my tongue.

Once lyrics have been chosen, sing the song with the students, enacting the movements related to each weather condition.

Extensions

It would be great if all students could contribute at least one idea and perhaps document their "songs" in a short book, decorated with their own artwork. This lesson could be modified for older grades as well; a lesson for older students could include a discussion on a wider variety of weather conditions, where each student has to contribute one part of the song or create her or his own song in its entirety.

Assessments

Using the Weather Worksheet, each student draws an image of the weather and states how it impacts the body—teacher should write in the student's spoken contribution.

Weather Worksheet	
Wind	**Snow**
Rain	**Sun**

Animal Rhythms

*Content Areas: Music, Science, Social Studies,
Visual Art*

Grade Level: First

Learning Objectives

1. Students will create instruments using art materials such as empty containers, construction paper, and paints.

2. Students will participate in a musical performance by playing with the instruments they create.

Standards

- National Standards for Music Education K–4
  - o Content Standard 2—Achievement Standards(a)(b)(c)
  - o Content Standard 6—Achievement Standard(c)
- National Standards for Early Childhood Education
  - o Standard 1(a)
  - o Standard 4(b)(c)

Procedures

Begin the lesson by reading the book *Jungle Drums* by Graeme Base. Discuss with students the various characteristics of animals, animal sounds, and the percussive beats and patterns in the book.

In order to make the instruments, students should have a variety of art materials to select from, including old food containers, empty cans, empty chips bags, empty coffee cans, etc. Additionally, provide students with various art mediums to decorate their instruments, including paint, construction paper, felt, crayons, pencils, or clay (or whatever is readily available).

Provide students with suggestions about materials they might use to represent some animals, such as *elephant*—gray, crumpled paper; *lion*—tan paper and brown yarn; *zebra*—black/brown stripes on white paper; *leopard*—small black spots on tan paper.

After all students have created their instruments, ask them to describe what animal sounds the instrument represents, what characteristics of sounds they hear and can make, and why they chose those sounds. Engage the class in an informal group performance, or ask students if they want to perform individually, in pairs, or in small groups.

Extensions

It is important here to keep the activity open-ended, as the focus is on creating sounds and instruments and not necessarily matching animal colors and characteristics.

Assessments

1. Document students' final products in a class display, or ensure that each child created an instrument and could describe a choice for animal sounds.

2. Students should be able to perform with their instruments or share the sound the instruments make.

Sounds of the Storm

Content Areas: Music, Science, Visual Art

Grade Level: Second

Learning Objectives

1. Students will identify the sounds of four different storms— thunder, lightning, rain, and hail.

2. Students will create instruments that imitate each of the four storm sounds.

3. Students will describe the qualities of each element of a storm and their choices for the correlating instrument.

Standards

- National Standards for Music Education K–4
  o Content Standard 2—Achievement Standards(b)(c)
  o Content Standard 6—Achievement Standard(c)
- National Standards for Early Childhood Education
  o Standard 3(c)
  o Standard 4(b)
  o Standard 5(b)

Procedures

Have a class discussion about the different types of weather. Allow students to provide suggestions and create a list from their ideas. Build on this list by asking students what sounds they hear during the different types of weather conditions, such as When it rains, what do you hear? How does it sound? What does it look like?

Provide students with a variety of artistic materials and mediums to create their weather instruments. Students can decide to make four different instruments or one instrument that makes four different sounds. The focus is on replicating the sounds of the storm, so any materials that would imitate the sounds will be most useful.

Ask students for their input as well; they may have ideas such as using rocks or pebbles, sticks and cans, or tissue paper and plastic cups to build their instruments. Students should be able to imitate the sounds of a storm through their instruments and should be able to describe why they chose the materials they did and what characteristics of the weather conditions are demonstrated by their instruments.

Extensions

Ideally, working on these instruments individually will allow students a certain freedom and level of creativity to explore sounds. However, students can be grouped into fours or even pairs as they work on these instruments. The goal is to understand the dynamics of sounds, pitches, and patterns that are found in the weather, and, after recognizing those sounds, to be able to replicate them with handmade instruments.

Assessments

Teachers can use the Sounds of the Storm Rubric to assess student work.

Sounds of the Storm Rubric				
Student	Identifies characteristics of different weather conditions	Uses materials creatively and appropriately	Describes relationship between sounds of the storm and sounds in instruments	Comments
A				
B				
C				
D				
E				
F				
G				
H				
I				
J				

Recycled Sounds

Content Areas: Music, Science, Social Studies

Grade Level: Third

Learning Objectives

1. Students will identify the characteristics of recyclable and reusable materials.

2. Students will construct their own percussion instruments using various natural and recyclable materials.

3. Students will identify the source of their materials and the materials' original purposes, and they will describe how they modified the materials to create instruments.

Standards

- National Standards for Music Education K–4
  o Content Standard 2—Achievement Standards(a)(b)
  o Content Standard 6—Achievement Standards(b)(c)
- National Standards for Early Childhood Education
  o Standard 2(c)
  o Standard 3(a)
  o Standard 5(b)

Procedures

Begin the lesson by reading the book *Our Class Is Going Green* (Scholastic) (or have students take turns reading aloud), and have a discussion of what it means to "go green" and recycle materials in our environment. Students should create a detailed list of various recyclable materials in the classroom. If possible, students should also create a list of recyclable materials within their homes.

To build upon the idea of going green, present students with a few recyclable materials (newspapers, empty cans, milk cartons), and ask them to create ideas for what these materials could be used for now. Engage students in a discussion about creating "recycled sounds" and using these materials to create musical instruments.

Have the students gather materials from their own homes to create their instruments and bring the materials in to share with the class. Students should be able to describe their materials and how they plan to use them to create an instrument. To further build the science and music connection, students should be able to describe which instrument family—such as strings, horns, or percussion—their instruments belong to.

Extensions

Two great ways to document this process are to take "before" and "after" pictures so students show how they transformed used/recyclable materials into musical instruments, and to showcase students' creations through an informal performance or presentation.

Assessments

1. In a class discussion, students should be able to identify the qualities of recyclable materials and list some items that could be recycled.

2. All students should construct their own instruments with materials they gathered at home.

3. Students should be able to describe how they used the materials to create a musical instrument, what the materials were originally used for, and how they created sounds. A journal entry reflecting on the process could be a nice supplement for their musical creation.

In My Family

Content Areas: Music, Social Studies

Grade Level: Kindergarten

Learning Objectives

1. Students will identify the individuals who compose their families.

2. Students will contribute one line to a song about family.

3. Students will actively participate in the song by singing along.

Standards

- National Standards for Music Education K–4
  - Content Standard 1—Achievement Standards(b)(c)
  - Content Standard 4—Achievement Standard(b)
- National Standards for Early Childhood Education
  - Standard 2(c)
  - Standard 3(a)

Procedures

Begin a discussion with the students about family, what family means, and who some members of their family are. Create a list or chart, and as students provide examples, add their suggestions. Once all the students have contributed some ideas, present students with the idea that they will be creating a song about their own families. Each student will describe her or his family in one line to be added to a song about family:

Family Song (sung to the tune of "Happy Birthday")

In my family,
In my family,
There's _____,
In my family!

As an example, you can present your own family and sing the song for the students. As students add their lines, have the entire class repeat and sing along to familiarize them both with the tune and with the idea of the personalized song.

Extensions

Some students will have many family members, and the one line addition can get quite long! This is alright, as it will make it comical and challenging to fit all the family members into the time and space allotted. Another idea is to summarize all the family members of everyone in the class and sing one line about "our family" and "there's" all the different individuals. This would make a very, very long lyrical line but one that creates a collaborative experience.

Assessments

In the In My Family Worksheet, students should draw the members of their family and list/share/write the names that they contributed in their song. The teacher should write the names students contribute as needed.

In My Family
My family includes_____
AND ME!

White House Rap

Content Areas: Music, Social Studies

Grade Level: Second

Learning Objectives

1. Students will create a rap on what they could do if they lived in the White House.

2. Students will describe at least three different events that they might influence.

3. Students will perform their rap for the class.

Standards

- National Standards for Music Education K–4
  - Content Standard 1—Achievement Standards(b)(c)
  - Content Standard 4—Achievement Standard(b)
- National Standards for Early Childhood Education
  - Standard 1(c)
  - Standard 3(c)
  - Standard 4(c)

Procedures

Pose the question: What would it be like to live in the White House? Ask students to brainstorm and share some ideas. What would they do? What would they change? List some of the ideas that the class contributes, and present students with the concept that they are going to write their own "White House Rap."

Briefly explain the qualities of a rap song—that it is based on facts, is written in a style very similar to poetry (steady beats and rhyming words), and is very personal to the artist/performer.

Students will then write their own raps about what they would do if they lived in the White House. Each rap song should include at least three different events or ideas that the students would change, shape, or impact with their position in the White House. Additionally, students should try to relate their ideas to actual current events.

Here are some suggestions for building the rap:

If I lived in the White House, I would say . . .
If I lived in the White House, I would do. . . .
If I lived in the White House, there would be. . . .

Once the raps are written, each student should perform her or his rap. The songs should be brief (three or more lines) and do not need to have music or any accompaniment. Work with students to speak at a steady beat and tempo when they are ready to perform.

Extensions

An alternative to having each child perform individually is to put students together in pairs. Although each child should still write his or her own verses, the performance would be jointly done to alleviate performance anxiety or stress. When the two students perform together, they would speak alternating lines or verses.

Assessments

1. Students should completely write out their White House Rap lyrics.

2. In the song, students should discuss major current events or situations that are relevant and meaningful either locally, nationally, or at an international level.

3. The final performance should be an informal presentation and sharing of ideas and goals. Students should stand up and perform their raps in front of the class.

An Asian Occasion

Content Areas: Music, Social Studies

Grade Level: Third

Learning Objectives

1. Students will listen to excerpts of music from India, China, and Japan.

2. Students will describe the different musical styles, noting the distinct tones, features, and patterns.

3. Students will interpret how each type of music is representative of a specific country.

Standards

- National Standards for Music Education K–4
  - Content Standard 6—Achievement Standards(a)(b)(c)
- National Standards for Early Childhood Education
  - Standard 1(a)
  - Standard 2(c)
  - Standard 5(b)

Procedures

Begin by asking students what types of music they like to listen to and what they listen to at home. Is there any type of music that is particularly loved by their family? Anything from another country or in a different language? If possible, ask students to bring in examples of the different types of music they like, and play examples for the class (ensuring everything is age appropriate). Have a short discussion about what students hear in the music (beats, patterns, specific instruments) and what they think of when they listen to the music.

You should have three different musical excerpts selected (one representative of each country—India, China, and Japan). Play the music for the students, and have them guess where they think the music comes from and if there is any specific function or association with the music. Ask them to add some descriptive words about imagery that is evoked or how they feel.

In the discussions, draw upon the musical vocabulary presented earlier in this chapter to engage students in talking about music with correct terminology. Ask them to feel the beats and rhythms, identify patterns in the music, and describe what types of instruments they hear—do they think the instruments have strings, are they horns, etc.

If the selections you use have a singer, ask the students to describe the singing voice and singing style, and discuss why that type of vocal music is important to each specific culture.

Suggested resources: Putumayo Kids has a compilation of Asian melodies entitled *Asian Dreamland* (very slow moving, lullaby-style pieces). It should be noted though that most of the songs are from Japan. Other sources for Asian music include clips from iTunes (search for Indian or Chinese instrumental music) and other compilations of Asian music for children. Basically, the idea here is to have three distinct and different pieces for students to compare and discuss, so any variety of musical selections would work.

Extensions

This lesson can be modified to focus on music from different regions of America (such as country music in Nashville, blues in Chicago, and jazz in New Orleans), music from different regions of Europe (either classical or folk tunes), or simply music from around the world. The goal is to engage students in a discussion about what they hear and how they interpret it, and to talk about different musical styles. Music from students' families is a great resource as well.

Assessments

Have students complete a Venn diagram based on the class discussions and their own interpretations of the music. Students should use specific musical terminology and examples in the music to support their ideas.

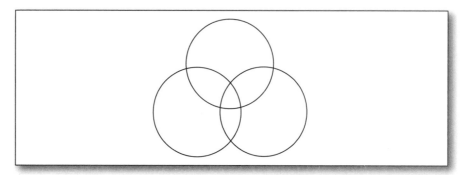

Hollywood and Bollywood

Content Areas: Music, Social Studies

Grade Level: Fourth

Learning Objectives

1. Students will listen to film songs from classic and contemporary Hollywood and Bollywood films.

2. Students will compare the music and lyrics, noting the cultural and contextual relevance.

3. Students will compare the role of film songs in each industry in historical and contemporary times.

Standards

- National Standards for Music Education K–4
  - Content Standard 6—Achievement Standards(a)(b)(c)
  - Content Standard 8—Achievement Standard(a)
- National Standards for Elementary Education
  - Standard 2(2.4)(2.5)
  - Standard 3(3.3)(3.4)

Procedures

While most everyone has heard of Hollywood and the American film industry, it is only in recent years that there has been a spotlight on Bollywood and the Indian film industry. Much of this has come from the appearance of Indian actors and actresses in American and British films, but more interesting is the fact that Bollywood produces nearly three times as many movies in a year as Hollywood produces. The name *Bollywood* is a combination of the name Hollywood with the name of the city at the heart of the Indian film industry, Mumbai (formerly Bombay).

Engage students in a discussion about songs in movies, asking them if they know of or can list any popular songs that they have heard in movies. Create a list of students' suggestions. Begin by discussing the role of songs and dance in Hollywood both in classical and contemporary times—what was the importance of songs in the movies of the 1940s (e.g., to uplift audiences during wartime) compared to songs in movies today?

Play audio clips of excerpts of songs, asking students to focus on the lyrics (perhaps give them a printout of the words in the songs), the instruments, and beats that they hear. Ask students what images the music evokes, if the songs are familiar to them, and what they imagine is taking place.

Continue the discussion by introducing Bollywood, the Indian film industry, and the relevance of "musical" style movies for Indian audiences. (Movies without songs often do not fare very well in India!) Play audio clips of songs, and ask students questions similar to those you asked about Hollywood songs: What do they believe the relationship is between the lyrics and the music? What is the context of the song in relationship to India's culture?

Here are some suggestions for songs and related discussions:

Classic Hollywood

"Singin' in the Rain" (from the film *Singin' in the Rain*): Discuss the impact of movie musicals for older audiences; these were geared toward presenting joyful, celebratory images during times of distress and war in America.

Contemporary Hollywood

"We're All in This Together" (from the film *High School Musical*): Discuss the shift in popular culture for musical style movies for younger audiences, based in part on the number of reality-based television shows focused on encouraging singers and performers.

Classic Bollywood

"Shree 420" (from the film *Ichak Dana Beechak Dana*): The song is set in a school where a teacher is singing to her students about creating and solving puzzles. This is a classic Hindi film, and this song is geared toward entertaining young children.

Contemporary Bollywood

"Ghanan Ghanan" (from the film *Lagaan*): Discuss this Academy Award nominated film about the sport of cricket and this song, which is set in a village that has struggled with drought for many months. The villagers cheer and celebrate when rain finally comes.

Extensions

Playing video clips of the songs is optional here, as students can describe the music and interpret the relationship between the lyrics and setting by just listening. Most of the clips are available without charge through various online websites and resources, if needed.

Assessments

The assessment for this lesson can be varied. Students can individually write their interpretations and comparisons, participate in a large class discussion, or work in small groups to present their understandings of the relationship between music, the movies, and the two cultures.

I Got the Blues

Content Areas: Music, Social Studies

Grade Level: Fifth

Learning Objectives

1. Students will compare and contrast five different African American musical artists and genres.

2. Students will identify the relationship between the music/lyrics and the time period in history.

Standards

- National Standards for Music Education 5–8
  - Content Standard 6—Achievement Standard(a)
  - Content Standard 9—Achievement Standards(a)(b)
- National Standards for Elementary Education
  - Standard 2(2.4)(2.5)
  - Standard 3(3.5)
  - Standard 4(4.0)

Procedures

Some of the most beautiful and inspiring music in American history was composed or influenced by African American artists. The music is often connected to specific regions in the United States (such as blues music in Chicago) or a particular time period and context (such as the work songs).

Begin a discussion with students by playing excerpts of the following songs. For each song, ask students to write down what images are evoked, what they believe the lyrics mean, what the context of the music is, and what the musical style is (if they can guess it).

Work song—"Pickin' Cotton All Day" sung by Creola Scott
Blues—"Why I Sing the Blues" sung by B. B. King
Jazz—"Cheek to Cheek" sung by Louis Armstrong and Ella Fitzgerald
Funk/soul—"I Feel Good!" sung by James Brown
Rap/hip hop—"Jump" sung by Kriss Kross

Engage students with questions about what they heard, what elements of the music stood out for them, and how they were able to distinguish or identify one musical style from another. Talk about some of the artists associated with the music, and ask students if they are familiar with any of the artists or musical styles. If they have heard the music someplace before, where or when did they hear it?

Students should also be able to relate each musical style to a period in history or geographical region. The discussion could lead to how each musical style originated in a particular area or why a musical style was important during a particular period of time.

Extensions

This lesson could actually take place over a week, with a focus on one musical style/song each day. The idea here is to have students recognize that music is often strongly connected with a place in history—either physically or socially—and the relevance of the songs to their place in history is as important as the meanings of the lyrics themselves.

Assessments

Two wonderful assessment ideas include placing students in small groups and having them either research one of the musical styles or create a presentation about the similarities and differences among the five different songs. Students could also write a paper or complete a verbal presentation, but this type of lesson lends itself well to researching historical facts and working collaboratively.

My Rhythmic Name

Content Areas: Music, Language Arts

Grade Level: Kindergarten

Learning Objectives

1. Students will identify the number of syllables in their name.

2. Students will chart the number of syllables in their name as an entire class.

3. Students will play the number of syllables in their name on an instrument as part of a class song.

Standards

- National Standards for Music Education K–4
  - o Content Standard 2—Achievement Standards(b)(c)
- National Standards for Early Childhood Education
  - o Standard 1(b)
  - o Standard 3(c)
- Common Core State Standards
  - o SL.K.6.
  - o L.K.2.

Procedures

Begin the lesson by gathering students in a circle. Explain to them that they are going to learn the rhythms in their names. As an example, state your own name (write it on the board or have it readily visible nearby), and clap the number of syllables as you speak your name. Demonstrate this example a couple more times, asking the students to clap the number of syllables with you.

Go around the circle stating each student's name and repeating the activity. Ask the students questions such as How many syllables/ beats do you think your name has? Can you try to find the rhythm in your name by clapping?

After all students have had a chance to recognize the number of syllables in their name, create a class chart with columns labeled from 1 to 9, and ask students which number their name fits under. For example, the name Kumar would go in the column labeled 2, because there are 2 syllables (beats) in the name Kumar.

As students are able to identify the number of syllables in their own names and grasp this concept, invite students to an informal presentation where the children perform their rhythmic names on instruments (or with hands, feet, etc).

Extensions

Build upon this lesson by having students practice the syllables and beats in the names of all their classmates. One idea is to clap, tap, or play a pattern that matches the beats in a student's name and see who can recognize their name! This can include the student's first and last name to increase the challenge.

Assessments

While class participation and aural recognition are the main assessments, having children complete a simple worksheet where they can use symbols or images to draw the number of beats in their name would be a great supplementary assessment.

Min-	Nie	Mouse
1	2	3
△	△	△

My Favorite Things

Content Areas: Music, Language Arts

Grade Level: First

Learning Objectives

1. Students will create their own lyrics to the song, "My Favorite Things."

2. Students will compare their favorite things with those of others in the class.

Standards

- National Standards for Music Education K–4
  - Content Standard 1—Achievement Standard(c)
  - Content Standard 4—Achievement Standard(b)
- National Standards for Early Childhood Education
  - Standard 1(c)
  - Standard 4(b)
- Common Core State Standards
  - RI.1.4.
  - SL.1.1.

Procedures

Begin the lesson by playing the song "My Favorite Things" from the musical *The Sound of Music.* (You can also show a short video clip of the song to facilitate discussion.) Ask students what some of the favorite things were that were listed. Why would those be the favorite things of the people singing the song? What does *favorite thing* mean? What are some of your favorite things?

As students share their ideas, write some down for the class to see a group list, and direct students to create their own lyrics to this song. Students should work in small groups with teacher assistance to create their own, shortened version of the song. Students should recognize that what they are writing first is poetry and that the words will then be sung to the music. Words such as *lyrics, rhyming,* and *melody* should be a part of the vocabulary for this lesson.

In their groups, students should then perform their songs for the class. (Each student can compose two lines, for example, to contribute to an entire song.) Chart the students' ideas by having students discuss and compare their favorite things: Were their things similar to or different from those of their peers?

Extensions

The goal here is for students to see the connection between the words in the song and the words as simple text—the connection between poetry and music. Any song can be substituted for this activity, but it should be one that engages students in a group and also allows for some individuality.

Assessments

While many first-grade students are still learning to read and write, the teacher can document the students' ideas. Some assessments include compiling a class song book or creating individual worksheets that students can decorate with art.

Classical Compositions

Content Areas: Music, Language Arts

Grade Level: Fourth

Learning Objectives

1. Students will research a composer from the Western classical music time period.

2. Students will identify the main components of the composer's life and identify the composer's most well-known works.

3. Students will reinterpret the composer's life by considering how the composer's success and contribution to the field would be different without those well-known works.

Standards

- National Standards for Music Education K–4
  - Content Standard 6—Achievement Standard(b)
  - Content Standard 9—Achievement Standards(a)(c)
- National Standards for Elementary Education
  - Standard 2(2.1)(2.5)
  - Standard 3(3.4)(3.5)
- Common Core State Standards
  - RI.4.9.
  - W.4.3.
  - W.4.7.

Procedures

Begin the lesson by playing a short excerpt of music (something from Mozart, Haydn, or Beethoven, so it reflects the classical time period). Ask students to talk about the music: What do they think of when they hear it? What does it sound like? What instruments do they hear?

Explain how this music is an example of Western classical music, which was written in a time period approximately from 1750 to the early 1800s. During this time, music was very structured and predictable, with recognizable patterns and orchestration.

Provide students with a list of composers to choose from (or assign them each a composer). Explain that they will conduct research to identify the main components of the composer's life and background, but they should focus more on specific successes and famous works. Finally, students will interpret how the composer's life might be different if he or she had not composed something that was so successful. Based on the composer's life, what other contributions might she or he have made to the field of music (or another field)?

The purpose is not only for students to recognize classical music and the significance of a specific composer to the field, but also to consider how classical music might be viewed differently today if some well-known compositions had not been written, or if the composer had not been as prominent during this time period.

Extensions

Western classical music remains the most commonly studied genre in the elementary music curriculum. This genre is the focus here to best align with what is currently taught in the schools and to take advantage of the resources that are most likely available. However, any musical time period (from any culture or country) could be the basis of this lesson. Students could research the life and times of a composer, artist, performer, or any contributor to the musical arts, with the same objectives and outcomes as those described here.

Assessments

While a written narrative is an obvious and logical assessment for this assignment, placing students in groups of three and having each one research one composer (or focus on one aspect of the project) provides opportunities for group work and collaboration. Students should also present a summary of their findings, including relevant music clips, to support their research.

A Cultural Connection

Content Areas: Music, Language Arts

Grade Level: Fifth

Learning Objectives

1. Students will interpret the song "My Paddle's Clean and Bright."

2. Students will describe how the time and place individuals live in impacts their culture.

3. Students will write their own folk song and describe a personal connection between the lyrics and their life.

Standards

- National Standards for Music Education 5–8
  - o Content Standard 6—Achievement Standard(a)
  - o Content Standard 9—Achievement Standard(a)
- National Standards for Elementary Education
  - o Standard 2(2.1)(2.5)
  - o Standard 4(4.0)
- Common Core State Standards
  - o RL.5.2.
  - o W.5.3.
  - o SL.5.4.

Procedures

One of the most well-known North American folk songs is entitled "My Paddle's Clean and Bright" and has been widely sung—as part of everything from large cultural celebrations to intimate campfires. The song is believed to have been written by Margaret Embers McGee in the early 1900s and is considered both a Canadian and Native American folk song. Some variations also include the word "keen" instead of "clean." The lyrics are simple and repetitive:

My paddle's clean and bright,
Flashing like silver
Follow the wild goose flight,
Dip dip and sway

Dip dip and sway it back,
Flashing like silver,
Follow the wild goose track,
Dip dip and sway.

Ask students to interpret the lyrics of the song. What do they mean? What are key words and phrases? How does the repetition impact the song? What are some ideas and images that are evoked by the song—a specific time and place, or something more general?

The song is typically sung in a round (where one person/group starts alone, and another joins in a few bars later, followed by another, until all persons/groups have sung the entire song twice). The rhythmic beat is also used for keeping a steady pulse when paddling a canoe.

Engage students in a discussion on the relationship between the song and a place (such as Canada or open lakes and mountains) or a culture (such as a Native American culture). Ask them to consider how the lyrics of the song show a connection to a specific time, place, or context.

Extensions

The steady and repetitive pattern of the song makes it simple to learn and perform. The lesson could be done without any music and as a study of the lyrics. Similarly, any folk song could be substituted here to build on the idea of analyzing relationships between the lyrics and the context within which the song was written.

Assessments

Students could work individually or in groups for this lesson. The focus should be on understanding the connection between the lyrics in the song (the meaning) and a specific culture, time, and place. Students can present their interpretations orally, write a paper, create a newsletter, or prepare a report in some other format that demonstrates their ability to recognize the connections between music and culture.

Students could also write their own folk song to show a deeper and more personal understanding of these connections. This assessment piece could focus on a time in their life, their environment, or their culture.

4

An Introduction to Theater

All the world's a stage.

—William Shakespeare

My first profession was as a performer. I studied music, theater, and dance; pursued a bachelor's degree in performance; auditioned for countless productions; and performed in a variety of shows and concerts on some of the largest stages in the United States. Yet, my greatest stage remains the classroom, because it is *my* stage.

I have often told teachers, administrators, and students that being a teacher is synonymous with being a performer. As an actress captures her audience in the first 5 minutes of a show, so too does a teacher draw in her students on the first day of class. As a performer delivers a written script with emotion and passion, so too is the teaching profession filled with prepared lessons, activities, and an unwavering love of our craft. Many teachers will attest to the idea that teaching is more than just a profession; it is a lifestyle, a way of being and thinking. Similarly, theater is more than just an art form, it is an expression of the human self, our inner being, and for that reason alone has the strongest connection with the art of teaching.

An Expression of Self

For even the youngest child, theater, drama, and role playing provide venues for self-expression, sharing and exploring feelings, problem solving, and understanding alternative perspectives. Yet, the experience of acting out and performing can also cause anxiety and stress, particularly for students who are unaccustomed to being in front of their peers. Around the age of six, children's cognitive skills develop dramatically as they increase self-awareness and perception, problem-solving skills, and a deeper understanding of their culture (Eccles, 1999).

In elementary school, children are in a developmental period referred to as middle childhood, which marks a time period when self-awareness, beliefs about self, and imaginative play emerge (Singer & Singer, 1990). Children develop a reflective self-awareness, which focuses on their awareness of themselves in relation to others (Modell, 2003). Children's ability to reflect not only assists them in recognizing their personal goals, but enables them to understand alternative perspectives. Recognizing their own feelings, which can be defined as the "private, mental experiences of an emotion," enables children to distinguish how others feel and perceive situations as they begin to understand their own feelings and perceptions (Damasio, 1999, p. 42).

Think back on your own feelings with respect to performance. Are you comfortable with public speaking? Does the thought of being in front of a large audience make you excited? Nervous? These are feelings we need to recognize as associated with theater, acting, drama, and role playing so that the activities that are presented to children are age (and situation) appropriate. It is also important to understand the origins of theater and the ways in which this art form made its way into the elementary school setting.

The earliest theaters, plays, and shows can be traced back to ancient Greece, where performers shared stories in theaters-in-the-round and various similar venues. Since those early days, theater has transformed to include much of what popular culture recognizes as the major forms of entertainment—film, television, and plays and other live performances—that define and shape our culture. Theater has also found a unique place within society through community theater, which began first as theater "by the people and for the people" and continues to hold a strong place in a variety of settings (Gard, Balch, & Temkin, 1968; Gard & Burley, 1959). Recently, theater has made a mark in our schools (primarily secondary schools) in afterschool programs, workshops, and several developing fine arts magnet programs.

Interestingly, theater is often the least common performing arts form to be integrated into elementary school settings by classroom teachers (Kindler, 1987; Mason, Thormann, & Steedly, 2004). In elementary schools and preprimary classrooms, theater is found in holiday concerts and shows, dramatic play centers, and role-playing activities. One of the most common ways that theater is integrated into the primary grades is through readers theater, a literary tool that provides students with expressive ways of developing language skills and reading fluency through practice and performance (Freedman, 1990).

Although an exact definition of readers theater varies in the literature, Millin and Rinehart (1999) define readers theater as "choosing something to read to an audience, practicing so that one can read the selection with accuracy and expression, and then reading the text for an audience" (p. 73). Through readers theater activities, elementary students experience the theatrical elements of spoken dialogue and live performance.

A culminating theatrical performance often functions as a positive learning experience for students. Jo Worthy and Kathryn Prater (2002) describe the importance of *practicing* for readers theater *performances*, stating that "as students learn what is needed to prepare for a successful performance, they are motivated to work and practice together productively" (p. 295). For students in the primary grades, readers theater fosters collaboration and introduces the experience of practicing, preparing, and completing a performance.

Importantly, integrated activities in theater can positively impact students' personal and social learning and increase their understanding of theater as an art form. Through theater, students become more focused and engaged, build their self-confidence and self-esteem, and hone cognitive skills such as memorization. Theater is a personal and collaborative art form that also fosters teamwork and cooperation. Additionally, there are several artistic skills that are integral to theater, such as vocal projection, expression when reading and delivering a script, an understanding of stage presence, and awareness of self on stage.

The personal, social, and theatrical skills that are fostered through integrated theater activities are summarized in Table 4.1 and serve as a foundation for the examples, vignettes, and lessons presented within this chapter.

Table 4.1	Learning Through Integrated Activities in Theater
Personal Learning	Focus, Motivation, Engagement, Memorization, Ownership of Work, Confidence, Self-Esteem, Understanding Alternate Perspectives
Social Learning	Cooperation, Building Friendships, Teamwork, Partner and Small Group Work
Theatrical Learning	Stage Presence, Voice Projection, Awareness of Self and Space, Awareness of Audience, Expression, Characterization

Integrating Theater

The ideas and suggestions for integrating theater into grades K–5 presented here are meant to be starting points for lessons and activities that have the most meaning within your own teaching context and curriculum. Some of the activities presented here are specific in their focus and connection to various subject areas, while others are broad and general, aimed at re-energizing your teaching and learning experience with your students.

Theatrical Autobiography

As you respond to the following prompts, please keep in mind the various names by which theater is known (e.g., drama, dramatic play, role playing, stagecraft, acting) so as to accurately reflect your own experiences and knowledge.

- My favorite experience with theater is . . .
- My earliest memory with theater is . . .
- My greatest challenge with theater is . . .
- My comfort level with theater is . . . because . . .

From these starting points, consider whether you have ever integrated theater (in any form) into your classroom. If you have, why did you choose to do so? Was it a movie you played for your students? Or a field trip to a live performance? If you have not, why not? Were you hesitant to integrate this art form? Uncomfortable with the idea of acting and performance?

These are all important, self-reflective questions that should be considered before integrating theater into your classroom. Integrating theater is not just about recognizing the value of this art form; it is also about the value for your *students*—the impact that these experiences will have on their personal, social, and academic learning.

The Process of Integrating Theater

While many teachers, parents, and administrators very well recognize the value of theater for children, the question often asked is, How do you begin to integrate theater into the classroom? The first place to start is to familiarize yourself with the theater standards. Some of the basic elements of theater include acting, improvisation (acting on the spot), role playing, building a scenario or scene, directing a scene or play, telling a story, interpreting a situation, and understanding the role of theater in various communities, cultures, and contexts.

Begin with what you have to teach in your classroom—a mandated curriculum, a unit that is the focus of the week, a schoolwide theme—and build theater into the existing activities. For example, if the entire school has adopted a theme of "Going Green" for spring, perhaps second-grade students can act out the life cycle of a tree, fourth-grade students can collaborate to write a short play on how they can impact the earth, and fifth graders can improvise various scenarios on making earth friendly choices.

One of the best ways to integrate any art form is with the introduction of relevant vocabulary. A great, ongoing activity is to connect these words and ideas into everyday contexts, so that students are building their vocabulary onto concepts that they are already familiar with. For example, when reading a story aloud, explain who the characters are, what that term means, and how it is relevant to theater. Can the students enact a story as the characters? Yes! Can the students rewrite the story by creating new characters? Absolutely. These are meaningful ways of introducing this terminology into existing vocabulary.

Building Artistic Vocabulary

Characters: The people who carry out the story and action, often through the use of verbal communication

Children's Theater: A formal, dramatic production that is directed and performed for children

Cooperative Work: The ability to work with a group and adjust personal needs and ideas to the process

Creative Drama: An informal technique that includes spontaneous acting without rehearsals and props

Focus: Staying on task and involved in the dramatic activity

Improvisation: The process of creating dialogue (and scene) in the moment

Projection: During speak or singing, sending the voice out into the audience (particularly important when not using microphones)

Script: The (written) document that outlines the characters, plot, and story

Sociodramatic Play: Play in which children imitate actions they have observed or experienced in their lives, modeling real-life experiences

Stage: The area, platform, or section of a room designated for performance

Thematic-Fantasy Play: Solitary or group play in which children engage on subjects that are imaginative, reflecting fantasy places and times

Vignettes and Viewpoints

One of the most valuable teaching tools that I have found in my experiences as a student, performer, and teacher is to consider examples from actual teaching practice and naturalistic observations. After reading through each vignette, consider your own viewpoint with the following questions:

- Is this an example of theater, dramatic play, or role playing?
- Can this scenario/activity be integrated into my own teaching context?
- What would my students learn from this experience?
- How would I assess a student's personal, social, and theatrical learning?

Mrs. S creates a research project for her third graders in which students will research and present a narrative report on an individual who inspires them most. In her class, the students' selections include a broad range of famous people, including Charlie Chaplin, Michael Jordan, Hilary Clinton, and Cleopatra, as well as others who are less well known, such as the mother, father, or grandparent of the student.

As a focus of this project, students have to dress up as the person they selected so as to fully embody the dynamics, character, and personality of their inspiring individual.

As Halloween approaches, it becomes apparent that many younger children choose to wear their costumes at all times of the day for several days prior to the holiday. At the grocery store, I see a six-year-old girl dressed up as a princess, wearing heeled shoes and a glittering crown. In my classroom, two seven-year-old boys (best friends!) insist on wearing fireman costumes (with hats and matching hoses) to school every day for a week. Not all students in the class dress up every day, but the appearance of these two boys sparks much conversation about who is wearing what costume, whether they will celebrate Halloween, and whether they are too old to go trick-or-treating.

In the front of the schoolyard at the end of the school day, three boys and one girl are playing together, running in the grass. One boy suddenly pauses and declares that he is going to start a rock band. He picks up a stick and imitates a guitarist, swinging his head in circles. The other two boys similarly pick up sticks, one also imitating a guitarist while the other beats the ground as though it is a drum set. The girl grabs a stick for herself and starts singing, twirling in circles to their imaginary, rhythmic beat.

As part of a small group activity, four first graders are assigned to work together to research the solar system. After facilitating and guiding their discussion, Mr. K suggests to the students that they imagine they are space explorers traveling to different planets. The first graders are thrilled with this idea and begin assigning themselves names, identifying favorite foods, deciding on favorite planets, and determining who will drive the spaceship. The students decide to research the solar system and present their work as these self-assigned characters.

Theater Activities for Transitions and Tensions

Elementary school days are a time when children are exploring and defining their own identity, seeking to be accepted by their peers and the adults in their lives. Importantly, it is a time period where children need nurturing, expressive outlets, and opportunities to explore creativity. In this section, I have listed three popular activities that are used by theater professionals in various contexts.

Each activity is modified to be appropriate for students in elementary school and is accompanied with an explanation of the specific theater skills that are being reinforced. Importantly, each of these activities fosters personal learning (focus, memorization, engagement) and social learning (working in partners, small groups, and large groups) through theater. Your students will cherish these activities as opportunities for transitioning from one lesson to another, to focus their minds in the morning, or to release some tensions later on in the day.

Sharing Emotions

Stand in a large circle as a class. Begin by sharing the emotion that you are feeling today, first with your facial expressions, then in body language, and finally by saying your name in a way that reflects your feeling. (For example, if you are angry, you might scrunch up your face, show tension in your body by making fists or stamping your legs, and then scream your name.) Each student should take a turn, but students may pass first and then contribute at a later time.

Skills—This activity teaches students to recognize their emotions and the ways that others are feeling. Students are encouraged to express themselves physically and verbally in a controlled, collaborative setting.

How Does It Feel?

In a small or large group setting, set up a scenario that involves a specific feeling (such as a student feels lonely when not included in a game, or a student feels angry at another person). Designate roles for students, and ask them to act out or role play the scenario. (This would work well if you model first with another teacher, parent volunteer, or student in the classroom.) The rest of the class should be the audience. At the end of the role playing, ask the students who were actors how it felt to act out the situation and what they believe the characters in the scenario could do differently. For those in the audience, ask what they observed and how they think each character in the scenario felt.

Skills—Children relate the most to their own feelings. Role playing encourages children to recognize their own feelings, understand alternative perspectives, and consider how another individual may feel in a similar situation.

Zip Zap Zop

Stand in a large circle as a class. As the leader of the activity, point your hand (by extending your entire arm out) to one student in the circle, and say the word "zip." The student who you pointed to continues by pointing a hand to someone else in the circle and saying "zap." That student then points a hand to another student and says "zop." This pattern continues, with each student saying one word in the order of the patter (zip, zap, zop), until someone says the wrong word, speaks out of sequence, or simply blanks out. (It happens!) Some challenging variations on this activity are to speed up the sequence or continually point to the same person. To decrease the difficulty level, you could also use a sequence of three words that is more familiar to students, such as tic, tac, toe.

Skills—This activity (which is quite popular in theater classes) teaches focus, engagement, concentration, and collaboration. In order to participate effectively, students have to focus intensely on who is pointing to whom and what word is said in the sequence. Note: This is a thrilling game that can be exhausting after having played a few times in a row.

What's the Problem?

Create a range of diverse and "realistic" scenarios that students may experience in the classroom and at home. Some suggestions are (1) a group of students cannot decide who should be the leader of an activity, (2) students do not want to follow classroom guidelines, and (3) a group of students cannot agree on the type of pie to bake as a class. Ask students to alternate in the roles of problem solvers and audience members.

Skills—This activity establishes role playing and dramatic play as a classroom activity so that all children are involved and encouraged to actively participate. This also creates a sense of community as students are observing their peers and acting out different scenarios.

Lessons and Assessments

While theater can be integrated into the classroom in the form of reflective tools and transitional games, it is a greater challenge to connect theater with academic subjects and an existing (often demanding!) curriculum. Here, I aim to address the needs and challenges that have been shared with me by teachers in many different educational settings by providing 16 examples of integrated theater lessons.

For each lesson presented in the following section, I have included learning objectives; standards for theater education, early childhood, and elementary educators; specific procedures for implementing the lesson, extensions to the activity, and assessments. There are a variety of assessments that can be used to assess the arts (such as performance assessments, work samples, portfolios, and video and audio documentation), but to make these lessons practical and applicable to your teaching contexts, I include assessments that are focused on meeting the learning objectives, but they could be easily modified. You will find that for each learning objective, there is a corresponding assessment.

The standards presented for each lesson are taken from the National Standards for Theater Education and include the appropriate standards and required knowledge for students in Grades K–4 and 5–8 learning contexts.

Each lesson is connected to the relevant core standards for early childhood education and elementary education and to the Common Core standards for math and language arts. By including these standards, I hope to continue the circle of self-reflection and professional development that is maintained throughout this book, so you may find the ways in which the students on your classroom stage can find their voice.

Puppet Power

Content Areas: Theater, Math, Visual Art

Grade Level: Kindergarten

Learning Objectives

1. Students will create their own puppets using specific shapes and patterns.

2. Students will create a short story correlating their own feelings to their puppets.

3. Students will identify the various shapes and patterns that compose their puppets.

4. Students will identify the relationship between puppetry and theater.

Standards

- National Standards for Theater Education K–4
  - Content Standard 2—Achievement Standard(a)
  - Content Standard 7—Achievement Standard(a)
- National Standards for Early Childhood Education
  - Standard 1(a)
  - Standard 3(c)
- Common Core State Standards
  - K.G.2.
  - K.MD.3.

Procedures

Share with students the idea that they will be making their own puppets. Ask students if they have ever seen or used a puppet. Why do we use puppets? What animals, people, places, images, shapes, and patterns can we find on puppets?

Explain a brief history of puppetry to students: Puppetry is a form of theater where puppets are used to perform a script, play, or musical. Puppets are believed to have been used for over 25,000 years and are found in some form in nearly every culture. Puppets are used in the musicals *The Sound of Music* and *Carnival!* and are found in Jim Henson's *Sesame Street*.

Present students with examples of puppets (either through simple puppets or more intricate examples associated with books or movies). Have students take time to explore puppets noting the colors, textures, and patterns.

Reiterate that puppets were originally used in theater during plays and shows as characters to tell a story. Gather students to discuss what shapes and patterns they notice on the puppets you share with them, and document their responses.

Provide students with a base for making their own puppets (e.g., a brown paper bag, an oven mitt, a sock), and present them with materials (such as felt, construction paper, cotton balls, stickers, markers, crayons, glue) to create their own puppets. This activity can be open-ended or connected to a specific theme or unit (such as frogs, the farm, animals). Instruct students to continually focus on using different shapes and creating patterns. Once the activity is completed, ask students to share their puppets and choice of shapes and patterns with the class.

Extensions

Build on the use of puppets by making puppets for a variety of units and topics covered in your curriculum. Using puppets is a wonderful way for students to express themselves, tell a story, create their own characters, demonstrate their understanding of concepts, and take ownership of their work. Students can either take the puppets home to share with families or collect their creations for a classroom puppet corner.

There are many different children's books available that use finger puppets or hand puppets to tell the story.

Assessments

1. Students individually construct a puppet using the materials provided to them, explaining their understanding of why puppets are used in theater and how they can be used to tell a story.

2. Students create a short story about their puppet and share this verbally with either the teacher or the class.

3. Students fill out the Puppet Power Worksheet. (Explain the directions prior to distributing the worksheet.)

Puppet Power!

Draw the shapes you used to make your puppet:

How many of each shape did you use?

Circle   Square   Triangle   Rectangle

100th Day Celebration

Content Areas: Theater, Math

Grade Level: First

Learning Objectives

1. Students will individually brainstorm ideas for celebrating the 100th day of school.

2. Students will collaborate with peers to present a short play on how to celebrate the 100th day of school.

3. Students will predict what might take place in another 100 days.

Standards

- National Standards for Theater Education K–4
  - Content Standard 2—Achievement Standard(a)
  - Content Standard 7—Achievement Standard(b)
- National Standards for Early Childhood Education
  - Standard 1(c)
  - Standard 3(b)
  - Standard 4(a)(b)
- Common Core State Standards
  - 1.NBT.1.

Procedures

The 100th day of school is a wonderful occasion in the first-grade classroom. What are some ways to make this experience unique for your students?

Engage students in a brainstorming session to determine what they would like to do on the 100th day of school. Ask students to share their ideas and also reflect upon and document in their journals their individual hopes for this big day! Place students into small groups (ideally of three or four students), and encourage them to share their individual ideas and collaborate to present a short performance about how to celebrate the 100th day.

As each group presents its performance, the other students should be good audience members and support one another. Then they can vote on which group's idea they like the best. As an addition to this lesson, ask students to make predictions about what they imagine will take place within another 100 days, and count to 100 as a group.

Extensions

Extend the idea of the 100th day by asking students to notice sets of 100 items around the classroom, in the schoolyard, and at home. Have jars of candy or other small items, and ask students to guess which jar holds 100 items. Talk about movies, plays, or shows on Broadway that have been performed for 100 days, or stories that were written 100 years ago.

Assessments

1. Students will contribute to the class brainstorming session and provide individual suggestions (in their journals) for the 100th day celebration.

2. Students will actively participate in their group's presentation and performance.

3. Students will document a prediction in their journals for what might take place within the next 100 days.

Shaping the Stage

Content Areas: Theater, Math, Language Arts

Grade Level: Fourth

Learning Objectives

1. Students will identify and construct at least three shapes to contribute to the creation of a stage or set for classroom performances.

2. Students will work collaboratively to construct the stage and will independently reflect on their experiences.

3. Students will identify the characteristics of at least three shapes (their angles and areas) that compose the stage, and define the required vocabulary words introduced throughout this lesson.

Standards

- National Standards for Theater Education K–4
  - Content Standard 3—Achievement Standards(a)(b)
- National Standards for Elementary Education
  - Standard 1(1.0)
  - Standard 2(2.1)(2.3)(2.5)
  - Standard 3(3.5)
- Common Core State Standards
  - 4.G.1.
  - 4.G.2.

Procedures

In order to establish a performance space for the classroom (any size is appropriate based on your needs), introduce students to the idea of making their own stage for performances. Engage students in a class discussion on the purpose of a stage, where stages can be found, and who uses stages and why. Describe the need for having a stage and the purpose of the stage in the classroom. Since the students will be using the stage, they will construct all of the pieces of the stage, represented in various geometric shapes, sizes, and polygons. Students will work independently and collaboratively to measure and create platforms, performance spaces, and props that correlate with specific shapes, angles, and measurements.

Introduce and define relevant vocabulary in a class discussion, and then post all the words with their definitions on a board (or in an accessible book) for students to reference. Suggested terms include *angle, line, polygon, vertex, triangle, equilateral, isosceles, scalene, acute, obtuse, quadrilateral, rectangle, square, parallelogram, rhombus, trapezoid, pentagon, hexagon, heptagon, octagon, nonagon,* and *decagon.*

Extensions

Ask students to either begin or continue this assignment by identifying and recognizing the various shapes and polygons that compose their furniture, surroundings, and classroom environment. Encourage students to measure and share their findings (either as an in-school activity or at home with families).

Assessments

1. Students' active participation can be assessed through teacher observation and/or documentation of each student's contribution through photographs.

2. Students write in a reflective journal with prompts to complete (such as, "The most challenging part of constructing the stage was . . .") and a page to define each of the vocabulary words.

3. Students fill out the Shaping the Stage Worksheet.

Shaping the Stage Worksheet

Shape 1

Draw image. (Label all angles.)

Identify and list specific characteristics of this shape. (For example, if the shape is a triangle, describe what type.)

Describe the location and placement on stage of this shape.

Calculate the perimeter and area of this shape.

Meet the Mathematician

Content Areas: Theater, Math, Social Studies

Grade Level: Fifth

Learning Objectives

1. Students will research a mathematician from ancient Greece, India, China, or Italy who helped shape the field.

2. Students will identify specific characteristics of their assigned mathematician including name and gender, nationality, physical traits, contribution to the field of mathematics, and any specific achievements for which they are known.

3. Students will write a narrative report that describes the impact that the work of their assigned mathematician continues to have on the field today.

4. Students will present their collected information by acting/representing their assigned mathematician in front of the class.

Standards

- National Standards for Theater Education 5–8
  - Content Standard 2—Achievement Standard(a)
  - Content Standard 5—Achievement Standard(a)
- National Standards for Elementary Education
  - Standard 1(1.0)
  - Standard 2(2.3)(2.4)(2.5)
  - Standard 3(3.5)
- Common Core State Standards
  - 5.MD.1.

Procedures

As an opportunity for understanding how the field of mathematics took shape as it is today, present students with the opportunity to travel back in time to meet the mathematicians of ancient Greece, India, China, and Italy who helped shape this field of study today.

Share with students a list of mathematicians who were pioneers of their time, summarizing a short biography for each individual. Assign the students (or have them choose) a mathematician to research. Select from the following list, or add to the list as you deem appropriate. You may need to assign the same mathematician to more than one student.

Greece—Pythagoras, Euclid, Archimedes, Aristotle

India—Ramanujan, Brahmagupta, Panini, Bhascaracharya

China—Chang Tsang, Liu Hui

Italy—Fibonacci, Girolamo Cardano

Students will conduct their research independently, but a way to build a collaborative focus of this lesson is to organize students into small groups based on the country that their assigned mathematician comes from.

Emphasize the importance of the presentation. Although students are presenting information, they are to perform, not just read a presentation aloud. Providing a variety of sources (books, journals, articles, websites, videos) will help facilitate their researching experience.

Present students with a scenario—that there is a math problem everyone is trying to solve, or that there is a contest to see who can create a new math formula—and engage students in the collaborative process of creating a plot and situation for dramatization. This activity aligns with National Standard for Theater Education, Content Standard 1: Script Writing by Planning and Recording Improvisations Based on Personal Experience, Heritage, Imagination, Literature, and History. It also aligns with their Achievement Standard: Students collaborate to select interrelated characters, environments, and situations for classroom dramatizations.

Extensions

Explain to the students that it is as important to be an audience member as it is to be a presenter. Continue that part of their role as audience members is to watch each presentation/performance and to guess which student is representing which mathematician. Provide each student with a worksheet with all the students' names in one list and all the mathematicians in a corresponding list. After all the presentations have been made, compare lists to see who identified all the mathematicians accurately!

Assessments

1. Students take research notes and write journal entries.

2. *My Mathematician Book*—Create a template for a book (simply fold and staple printer paper to resemble a book), and label each page in the book (six pages in total). On the first five pages, students provide the information for their mathematician listed in Learning Objective 2 (name and gender, nationality, physical traits, contribution to the field of mathematics, and specific achievements), and the sixth page should include relevant and specific mathematic terms relating to measurement and quantity.

3. Students write a narrative report, at least two pages in length.

4. The class presentation can be assessed with the Meet the Mathematician Rubric for performance and presentation of information.

Meet the Mathematician Rubric			
Grading Criteria	*1*	*2*	*3*
Research	Research was minimal, and several elements were missing.	Research was detailed, but a few required elements were missing.	Research was thorough, detailed, and appropriate.
Presentation	Student did not adequately address the class and was unprepared for the presentation.	Student addressed the class but was unfocused or unprepared at times.	Student addressed the class directly and was expressive in the presentation.
Performance	Student did not accurately represent the assigned mathematician in the performance.	Student represented the assigned mathematician minimally through physical traits, expression, and/or apparel.	Student accurately represented the assigned mathematician through physical traits, expression, and/or apparel.

Outer Space

Content Areas: Theater, Science, Language Arts

Grade Level: First

Learning Objectives

1. Students will improvise scenarios in "outer space" through a series of prompts.

2. Students will work collaboratively in groups of three.

3. Students will create their own scenarios noting specific and appropriate characteristics of being in outer space.

Standards

- National Standards for Theater Education K–4
  - o Content Standard 1—Achievement Standard(a)
  - o Content Standard 4—Achievement Standard(a)
- National Standards for Early Childhood Education
  - o Standard 1(c)
  - o Standard 4(b)
  - o Standard 5(b)

Procedures

As students are learning about objects in outer space (such as planets, meteors, moon, sun, shuttles, astronauts), engage students in a dramatic activity of improvisation where they will use their knowledge of outer space to find creative solutions to a variety of prompts and scenarios.

Begin by defining and explaining the concept of improvisation and explaining how improvisation is used by professional actors both in practice and performance. During improvisation, all actions and choices are acceptable, but the goal is to think of "realistic" and creative solutions to the scenarios presented. With improvisation, you have very little time to prepare. Instead, you "think on your feet." Here are some examples to start:

> *You just landed on the moon.*
> *Your spaceship was hit by a meteor.*
> *You and your crew discover a new planet.*
> *You have a friendly encounter with aliens.*
> *You return to earth—tell the news reporter what you experienced.*

The main purpose is to encourage students to participate in the activity. The prompts can be changed or rewritten based on the content you are currently teaching in your class. Encourage the students who are audience members to be supportive of their peers and think of their own solutions to the scenarios they are watching.

Ask students to create their own prompts also, perhaps directing their peers by presenting a scenario for them to improvise.

Extensions

This would be a wonderful activity to document (either in written form or through videotapes). Consider continuing the activity of improvisation in another subject area. Many local performance halls (such as Second City in Chicago), community centers, and children's theater programs regularly have performances based around improvisation. Consider taking your students on a field trip to view professionals engaged in improv.

Assessments

1. Teacher observes that each student actively participated in the improvisation scene.

2. Each student contributed at least one dialogue or solution to the scene.

3. Students documented their own ideas in a journal or shared their scenarios with the class.

Digging to Discover

Content Areas: Theater, Science, Language Arts

Grade Level: Second

Learning Objectives

1. Students will act as paleontologists, botanists, or fossil hunters to find hidden materials in the classroom.

2. Students will identify species of dinosaurs based on their groups' findings.

3. Students will document their findings on the Digging to Discover Worksheet.

Standards

- National Standards for Theater Education K–4
  - Content Standard 1—Achievement Standard(a)
  - Content Standard 2—Achievement Standard(c)
- National Standards for Early Childhood Education
  - Standard 1(c)
  - Standard 2(c)
  - Standard 3(a)(b)

Procedures

In preparation for this lesson, select five or six dinosaurs that will be the focus of the lesson. (You should select one dinosaur for each group of four students in your class.) Gather or create images of small footprints, claws/nails, fossils of animals and plants, and any other items that can be easily related to a specific species of dinosaur.

Place students into groups of three, assigning each one a role: paleontologist, botanist, or fossil hunter. Designate specific tasks for each student in the group. (Asking students what they think their role should be would be a great idea as well.)

Explain to students that they will be "digging to discover dinosaurs" that are hidden throughout the classroom. Each group (designated by colors) will have to track down and find the materials for their assigned dinosaur. Once they find the materials, students are each responsible for sorting and categorizing the materials (based on their assigned roles), listing the materials, and collaborating with their group to identify the species of dinosaur and the time period in which it lived.

Note: The method by which students have to "find" their dinosaur should be related to the classroom setup and materials available. Ideally, students can have the opportunity to act out their roles as paleontologists, botanists, and fossil hunters through interpreting clues, messages, or a "treasure hunt" to find their dinosaur.

Extensions

If the weather permits, this activity would be a wonderful exploration outdoors. Students could really "dig" to find fossils, bones, and other materials representing prehistoric times. Build on the role-playing aspect of this lesson, asking students to consider what other kinds of professionals play an important part in finding and preserving fossils and dinosaur bones.

Additionally, any lesson that focuses on dinosaurs definitely calls for a field trip to the local museum or community center! Many of these settings also lend supply boxes to teachers for use in classrooms. This would also be an ideal resource for materials for this lesson.

Assessments

Students' active participation in their assigned group roles should be documented through teacher observations. Students should use the Digging to Discover Worksheet to record their identification of the species they have discovered based on the materials their group uncovered.

Digging to Discover

Name:

My role in the group:

Materials found (list each individually):

Time period (circle one and explain why):

Triassic   Jurassic   Cretaceous

Identify the species of dinosaur you have discovered:

Famous and Fabulous

Content Areas: Theater, Science, Social Studies

Grade Level: Third

Learning Objectives

1. Students will research a scientist or inventor who made an important contribution to the field.

2. Students will collect their information and create a presentation for the class.

3. Students will perform in the role of their selected scientist or inventor through the use of costumes, speech inflections, or a scientific demonstration.

Standards

- National Standards for Theater Education K–4
  o Content Standard 2—Achievement Standards(a)(b)
  o Content Standard 5—Achievement Standard(a)
- National Standards for Early Childhood Education
  o Standard 3(a)(b)
  o Standard 4(b)
  o Standard 5(b)

Procedures

As part of any elementary science curriculum, students are required to study various scientists and inventors whose discoveries and creations made significant contributions to our culture and society. Present students with the idea that not only will they be selecting and researching an individual, they will also be performing their findings in character for the class. They can conduct their research using sources already collected by the teacher or any other sources that are age appropriate for the students. Explain the guidelines—that the researched information needs to be accurate, the findings have to be collected from various sources, and the presentation should be a performance where the student speaks, dresses, acts, or demonstrates an activity that best represents their selected individual.

Encourage students to research a scientist or inventor who discovered something that they find interesting, such as the creator of bubblegum or the person who first used a telescope. (Notice that the inventor of chocolate milk is on this list!) Here is a suggested list of scientists and inventors:

Albert Einstein

Bartolomeo Cristofori

Benjamin Franklin

Charles Darwin

Coenraad Johannes
van Houten

Galileo Galilei

Henry Ford

Isaac Newton

Isaac Singer

Johann Gutenberg

John Pemberton

Louis Braille

Marie Curie

Roger Bacon

Thomas Alva Edison

Wilhelm Rontgen

Extensions

The research gathered from this lesson would make a wonderful presentation for families and friends. Consider creating a scientist or inventor day where students present their research in character and perform their findings for a much larger audience.

Assessments

1. Students individually select and research a scientist or inventor to study.

2. Students gather information from a variety of sources, including books, magazines, and websites.

3. Students create a short performance as their selected scientist or inventor and present their findings in character for the class.

Perfecting Our Potions

Content Areas: Theater, Science, Language Arts

Grade Level: Fourth

Learning Objectives

1. Students will create their own experiments and potions by writing about the process of selecting ingredients and creating a recipe.

2. Students will hypothesize the results of their classmates' potion recipes after hearing what the ingredients are.

3. Students will share their creations and findings in a class performance or science fair and contribute their potion recipes to a class project.

Standards

- National Standards for Theater Education K–4
  - o Content Standard 1—Achievement Standard(a)
  - o Content Standard 2—Achievement Standard(c)
- National Standards for Elementary Education
  - o Standard 1(1.0)
  - o Standard 2(2.1)(2.2)(2.5)
  - o Standard 4(4.0)

Procedures

There is a magic and mystery to potions—how they were used and what they were used for. Much of the mythology and literature describes how wizards and witches, magicians, sorcerers, and fairies created these magical elixirs. Potions were believed to cure ailments and illnesses, create love or death, or make a person fall asleep or gain superhuman strength.

Ask students: Imagine what type of potion you would make, if you could make one! What ingredients would you put in your potion? How much of each ingredient would you need? Would this be a powerful potion or something mild, something in a large bottle, or just an eyedropper?

Present students with the premise that they are going to be creating their own potions. Students can take on any role that they choose (either a fantasy role or a realistic one—such as that of a doctor or scientist) and need to use materials and liquids that are related to the roles they have chosen and the effects the potions are to have. For example, a student who is creating a sleeping potion might include feathers from a down pillow. Students will then present their potions (in character) to the class, when other students will hypothesize what each potion is supposed to do. The final products can be shared at a science fair or potions performance and documented in a class book.

Note: Based on the topic or theme or your current science unit or lessons, you should specify a required component in the students' potions (a specific element, liquid, or solid) to encourage continuity with the topics covered in your class.

Additional Sources:

Alice's Adventures in Wonderland, by Lewis Carroll

Harry Potter (series), by J. K. Rowling

The Encyclopedia of Fantasy (St. Martin's, 1997), by John Grant and John Clute

Extensions

An additional discussion could be had during this lesson on the topic of alchemy as a mythological and scientific practice, often considered a precursor to chemistry. The idea of creating a potion and taking on a role can be modified to fit many different science topics. Students can create their own plant or animal species, invent a new type of weather system, or develop their own element for the periodic table.

Assessments

1. Students will write and document their potions recipes with ingredients and step-by-step directions.

2. During the class performance, each student will hypothesize what the effects of their classmates' potions will be, based on the ingredients in the potions. Students must note what materials in each recipe supported their hypotheses.

3. Each student's final potion recipe will be documented in a class book, newsletter, or display.

My Many Faces

Content Areas: Theater, Social Studies

Grade Level: Kindergarten

Learning Objectives

1. Students will create masks that demonstrate various feelings, including happy, sad, excited, angry, and tired.

2. Students will describe the characteristics of each mask by drawing comparisons between their own feelings and the images on each mask.

3. Students will "wear" a mask each day by selecting a mask that best represents their feelings for the day.

Standards

- National Standards for Theater Education K–4
  o Content Standard 7—Achievement Standard(a)
- National Standards for Early Childhood Education
  o Standard 1(c)
  o Standard 5(b)

Procedures

As students augment their communication skills and develop an awareness of others, they are building their capacity to recognize and describe their own feelings.

Beginning this lesson with a book on feelings is a great hook to start the discussion. Additionally, present students with the statement: When I am at school, I feel . . .

Ask them to complete the sentence. Have a discussion on each student's stated feeling, asking Why do you feel that way? What is a time when you feel differently?

Masks are a common part of theater in many different cultures and contexts. Perhaps most famous is the duality of the Greek comedy and tragedy masks. Ask students, Why would someone wear a mask? What can you tell about the way a person feels from the mask?

Share various pictures and images of masks (and real ones if you have access to them), so students can discuss the purposes of masks, how masks are useful, and how the students might use masks to share their own feelings.

Engage students in the process of making their own masks, explaining that each student will create four masks to represent four different feelings. The students will then describe how they chose the features for their masks, and each morning they will select a mask that best represents how they feel that day.

The materials for this lesson can vary. The masks can be made out of paper bags, construction paper, cardboard, or cardstock and glued onto popsicle sticks or straws. The tools and materials for decorating the masks can be something as simple as crayons and markers, or they may include more elaborate accessories such as glitter, stickers, felt balls, or feathers. The goal is for students to recognize the purpose of masks in theater—a means of sharing feelings and expression—and to find a way to document their own feelings in their masks.

Note: Create a designated area in the front of the classroom for students to store and display their masks. Each day when students enter, they should select a mask that best represents how they feel. By specifying a place for the unused or unchosen masks, you provide students with the option of alternating their feelings throughout the day, and take ownership over this activity each morning.

Extensions

Feelings are a very important topic in kindergarten; they are covered in class discussions, books, individual lessons, and art activities. Build on this topic of feelings throughout the classroom. Starting with the masks, create other centers and areas where students can explore and express their feelings. Since many kindergarten classrooms are typically arranged with centers and manipulatives, create a specific focus for use of the different centers, such as listening to songs about feelings or reading books on feelings.

Assessments

1. Each student should create at least four different masks using the materials provided. Each mask should depict a different feeling (such as happy, sad, excited, angry, tired, or hungry).

2. Ask students to verbally share information about their masks either with the teacher in a one-on-one conversation or in a larger class discussion. Students should note specific characteristics in each mask that represents how *they* feel.

3. Students should select a mask in the morning and place the mask next to their names (on their name card or locker). The selection of the mask is a way for students to communicate how they feel each day and can lead to a brief discussion every morning.

Solving the Scenario

Content Areas: Theater, Social Studies, Language Arts

Grade Level: First

Learning Objectives

1. Students will improvise and develop their own character, decisions, and conflicts in a specific scenario.

2. Students will engage in collaborative role playing.

3. Students will observe their peers role playing in various scenarios and reflect on possible solutions to the problems presented.

Standards

- National Standards for Theater Education K–4
  - o Content Standard 2—Achievement Standard(c)
  - o Content Standard 5—Achievement Standard(a)
- National Standards for Early Childhood Education
  - o Standard 3(a)(b)
  - o Standard 4(b)
  - o Standard 5(b)

Note: Structured dramatic play is a natural and collaborative way to foster problem-solving skills. When solving problems within predetermined scenarios, students are encouraged to make choices and find solutions. Create a diverse range of realistic scenarios representing situations that students may experience in the classroom and at home. These collaborative experiences are invaluable for reinforcing classroom guidelines and social skills and for creating a safe environment where students can improvise, develop, and practice problem solving.

Procedures

Engage students in the process of role playing (structured dramatic play) by presenting a realistic scenario with a conflict that needs to be resolved. Assign students roles within the scenario, and facilitate a discussion as they consider the problem and provide their own solutions. (This activity, when initially introduced, works well when modeled first by the teacher, student teacher, assistant, or parent volunteer in the classroom.) For example, if you present students with a scenario where one student is being left out of a game, assign students roles within this scenario and encourage them to improvise a solution to the problem. (Some prompts or prompting questions are helpful!) Allow students to find their own solutions, and pause the improvisation as needed to ask the entire class to reflect on and describe the process.

As important as it is for each student to participate in the scenarios, it is just as important for each student to observe and act as an audience member. Inform students that they will be required to reflect independently in their journals on the scenarios that they observed. Students should be encouraged to write out their solutions to the problems either independently or with partners.

Scenarios for Initiating Structured Dramatic Play	
Suggested Scenarios	*Prompting Questions*
A group of children cannot decide who should be the leader of an activity.	How can we take turns?
A child does not want to share a new toy.	How do you feel when someone does not want to share with you?
Someone made a hurtful comment to another person.	What are some nice things to say to one another?
Children do not want to follow classroom guidelines.	Why is it important to have classroom rules?
A child feels left out of a small group activity.	How do you feel when you are not included?
One child does not want to participate in a game.	Why is it important to try new things?
A child is very angry at another person.	How you do feel inside when you are angry?
A group of children cannot agree on the type of pie to bake as a class.	What are some ways that we can make fair choices?
A child is nervous about performing in front of an audience.	How do you feel when you are nervous? Excited?

Extensions

While the suggested scenarios and prompting questions provided here are great starting points for engaging students in problem-solving and conflict resolution, ask students to share examples from personal experiences to augment this activity. Always be cognizant of the stories or scenarios students may present, keeping the activity age-appropriate, and maintaining the lesson as a platform for safe discussions.

Assessments

1. Students' improvisations can be assessed with the Solving the Scenario Rubric.

2. Teachers observe active and appropriate participation.

3. Students contribute to class discussions and write journal reflections.

Solving the Scenario Rubric			
Grading Criteria	*1*	*2*	*3*
Improvisation	Student's dialogue and actions were not appropriate or related to the scenario.	Student created somewhat appropriate dialogue and/or actions based on the scenario.	Student created appropriate dialogue and actions based on the assigned scenario.
Collaboration	Student did not effectively collaborate with the others in the scenario.	Student responded minimally to others in the scenario, improvising mostly independently.	Student worked collaboratively with others in the scenario, reacting to prompts, conversations, and actions.
Participation	Student was not engaged and did not participate in solving the scenario.	Student was minimally engaged and participated minimally in solving the scenario.	Student was actively engaged and fully participated in solving the scenario.

Oregon Trail Mix

Content Areas: Theater, Social Studies, Geography

Grade Level: Third

Learning Objectives

1. Students will improvise scenes about the Oregon Trail by making choices when food and supplies become scarce.

2. Students will collaborate with peers to create improvised scenes in small groups.

3. Students will provide realistic, appropriate solutions based on the time and setting provided in the prompts.

Standards

- National Standards for Theater Education K–4
  - o Content Standard 2—Achievement Standard(a)
  - o Content Standard 5—Achievement Standard(a)
- National Standards for Early Childhood Education
  - o Standard 1(c)
  - o Standard 4(b)
  - o Standard 5(b)

Procedures

Introduce students to the concept of improvisation—acting spontaneously and thinking of words, ideas, and solutions "on the spot." Talk about why improv is challenging (pressure to think of ideas, having to focus, work with other actors) and how it is beneficial (helps focus, builds creativity and problem-solving skills).

In this lesson, students will improvise a scenario from the experiences of the travelers on the Oregon Trail. Each group of students (either three or four to a group) will have to improvise a scene and make a decision on how to handle the challenges that they encounter. Here are some suggested scenes:

> *Two parents and their two children are traveling by covered wagon. They have very little food left and two horses to feed. In their savings, they have only $10. In the nearest shop, they have to decide how much food to buy for themselves and how much to buy for their horses.*

Three brothers (or sisters) are traveling by foot across the trail. They sold their broken wagon for $50 and have made a decision to buy four oxen at Fort Hall. The brothers (or sisters) also have to consider how much money to spend on food and water for themselves, and how much, if any, money they should save.

Two friends are traveling by horse on the trail and meet two travelers whose wagon has a broken wheel. The travelers ask to join the friends on their path and offer to pay for the expenses of the trip. Including food and water for all the people and the horses, how much should the travelers pay? Should the friends let the travelers join them?

Prior to this lesson, students should have a concrete understanding of the Oregon Trail and the purpose, challenges, and goals of the individuals making this arduous journey. Many families traveled with young children and animals, taking all their belongings from the Midwest over to the Oregon Territory.

Students' responses and ideas in the improvised scenes should be realistic, related the scenario, and appropriate for the setting and challenges presented.

Extensions

The idea here is to continue on the thread of problem solving and encourage students to improvise scenes and solutions of real, historical events. Modifying the subject matter here is an easy variation. The topic of this improvisation does not have to be the Oregon Trail; rather, it can be any subject, theme, or topic that is currently a part of your curriculum.

Assessments

1. Students' participation is as actors in scenes. Each student should participate in at least one scenario.

2. The responses given should be related to the ideas presented within the group, showing that each student is collaborating through improvisation.

3. Students' responses and ideas in the improvised scenes should be realistic, related to the scenario, and appropriate for the setting and challenges presented.

It's Fine to Pantomime

Content Areas: Theater, Social Studies

Grade Level: Fourth

Learning Objectives

1. Students will explore the art of pantomime by depicting an event in American history.

2. Groups of three students will create scenes to perform for the class.

3. Students will participate as audience members to guess the event or story pantomimed by their peers.

Standards

- National Standards for Theater Education K–4
  - o Content Standard 2—Achievement Standard(a)
  - o Content Standard 5—Achievement Standard(a)
- National Standards for Elementary Education
  - o Standard 1(1.0)
  - o Standard 2(2.4)(2.5)

Procedures

Recognizing and understanding events in American history is an important part of the upper elementary curriculum. Most often students read about, memorize, and then write about these events. To build on the importance of these events that shaped American history, engage students in the activity of *pantomime,* or acting without words. Give a small group of students a specific event that they have to pantomime, and have the class guess what event the group is representing. Below is a suggest list of dates and events:

1492: Christopher Columbus lands in what is now the Bahamas.

1607: Pocahontas saves the life of John Smith.

1759: Benjamin Franklin invents the lightning rod.

1776: In July, the 13 colonies sign the Declaration of Independence.

1789: George Washington becomes the first president of the United States of America.

1804–1806: Meriwether Lewis and William Clark travel overland from Saint Louis, Missouri, to the Pacific Coast and back.

1860: Abraham Lincoln becomes president of the United States.

1869: The transcontinental railroad is completed.

1879: Thomas Alva Edison perfects the electric light bulb.

1908: Ford Model T mass-produced automobile is introduced.

1927: Charles Lindbergh flies across the Atlantic Ocean.

1964: The Beatles arrive in America.

The premise of this lesson is very similar to that of popular games that require individuals to share an idea or clue without talking about the specific subject. The students in each group or pair should collaborate briefly to plan how they will act out their event, and after the performance, class members should document their educated guesses in their journals.

Extensions

Pantomiming is one of the oldest forms of theater—used by mimes and actors with masks in a variety of cultures. The challenge here is to communicate specific details without speaking, using the body for expression and collaborating with other actors. Originally, pantomiming was a solo performance, so if your students have the confidence and opportunity, encourage them to try pantomiming an event (in any topic) on their own!

Assessments

1. Each group will collaborate and plan how the scene will be presented.

2. Every student in the audience has to guess what event is being pantomimed. The students can either use their prior knowledge of American history to draw upon for their guess, or be given a list from which to choose from prior to the activity.

In 1492, Who Found America, Was it You?

Content Areas: Theater, Social Studies

Grade Level: Fifth

Learning Objectives

1. Students will rewrite American history to create a new explorer who discovered America.

2. Students will work in pairs to create a script of the discovery, noting important facts such as the explorer's country of origin, crew members, mode of transportation, goals, and final discoveries.

3. Students will read their scripts aloud for the class with expression.

Standards

- National Standards for Theater Education 5–8
  - Content Standard 1—Achievement Standard(a)
  - Content Standard 4—Achievement Standard(a)
  - Content Standard 5—Achievement Standard(a)
- National Standards for Elementary Education
  - Standard 1(1.0)
  - Standard 2(2.4)(2.5)
  - Standard 3(3.5)

Procedures

Everyone knows how Christopher Columbus "discovered" America, but what if America had been "found" by someone else? What if a different explorer stumbled across this country; what could it be named? How might this new explorer have changed the course of America's development?

Columbus's discovery was not a simple undertaking; rather, it was the result of a large mission presented to him by the queen of Spain. With his large crew, three ships, and several individuals supporting his voyage, he found and named what we know today as America.

Challenge your students to create a new explorer, or take one from history and place him or her as the individual who discovered

America. What was the original purpose of this individual's journey? Where was this person trying to go? What country did this explorer originate from, and who were the fellow travelers? Did this happen in 1492 or in another time?

In groups of three to five, students will collaborate to brainstorm and write a short script about the discovery of America. Students need to designate characters and roles; write dialogue; create a setting, plot, and conclusion; and be prepared to read their scripts with expression for the class.

Extensions

This lesson will probably take at least a week of preparation and discussion with a final performance at the end of the week. The purpose of this lesson is to encourage students to write and perform their own script on a topic that is familiar and yet creative. The idea can easily be modified to any other subject area.

Assessments

1. Although students are writing their scripts in groups, this lesson could be turned into a written assignment where each student brainstorms his or her own explorer.

2. Each student will actively participate in writing and planning the script; taking on a role/character; and planning the scene, plot, setting, and conclusion.

3. Each group will read their script for the class using expression.

What's the Weather?

Content Areas: Theater, Language Arts, Science

Grade Level: Second

Learning Objectives

1. Students will create their own weather forecast for the week.

2. Students will predict the weather in three different regions of the country.

3. Students will act as meteorologists and share their forecasts with the class.

Standards

- National Standards for Theater Education K–4
  - Content Standard 1—Achievement Standard(a)
  - Content Standard 2—Achievement Standard(a)
- National Standards for Early Childhood Education
  - Standard 1(c)
  - Standard 3(a)(b)
  - Standard 4(b)
- Common Core State Standards
  - RI.2.3.
  - W.2.7.
  - SL.2.4.

Procedures

What is the weather today? Ask students how it looks outside. How does it feel? Is it the same or different from the weather yesterday, and what will the weather be like tomorrow?

Explain how meteorologists use various instruments to predict the weather, but before modern science and technology, people used the moon phases, changing seasons, and sometimes simple guesswork to create a weather forecast. Students should also read through teacher selected weather forecasts to gather an understanding of their scope and content.

Each student will document the weather for one week, noting the temperatures, cloud conditions, rain or snow, wind speeds, sunshine, and humidity. Students will then analyze the weather documented in their notes and predict how the weather will be for the following week. Each student will also select two additional regions or cities to create weather forecasts for (such as one on the East Coast, one in the central United States, and one on the West Coast).

Once each student has created a forecast, students will perform their predictions by acting as meteorologists. Students will share what they believe the weather will be like in the upcoming week and why they were led to these conclusions. Students can create visuals to support their forecasts. Students can have the option to write their notes out in detail or improvise their scenes based on the facts they noted.

Extensions

Depending on the amount of time allotted for this activity, students can track the weather either for a day or for an entire month before creating their own forecasts. Importantly, students should be writing specific facts about the weather so that they have concrete examples to refer to when making their predictions for the following week. Students may need some additional explanation on analyzing trends, in that if it is sunny all week and it is late spring, it is very likely to continue in that same manner.

Assessments

1. Students create individual weather forecasts based on their documentation of at least one day's weather related data or up to a week's worth of data.

2. Students specify the three regions for which they will be creating weather forecasts. (The students' current location should be included.)

3. Each student will perform as a meteorologist (similar to one they might see on television) as they share and explain their predictions.

My Story, My Voice

Content Areas: Theater, Language Arts

Grade Level: Third

Learning Objectives

1. Students will write their own autobiographies, focusing on important events and individuals in their lives.

2. Students will enact their autobiographies through a soliloquy (solo performance).

3. Students will recognize similarities and differences among their own stories and those of their peers.

Standards

- National Standards for Theater Education K–4
  o Content Standard 1—Achievement Standard(a)
  o Content Standard 2—Achievement Standard(a)
  o Content Standard 5—Achievement Standard(a)
- National Standards for Early Childhood Education
  o Standard 1(c)
  o Standard 2(b)
  o Standard 3(a)(b)
- Common Core State Standards
  o W.3.3.
  o SL.3.3.
  o SL.3.4.

Procedures

Explain to students that they will be writing their autobiographies—that is, detailing all the important events and people in their lives from birth until the current day. Students should start by brainstorming through a web or outline, highlighting important events, family outings, performances, or sports events as well as favorite movies, songs, and activities.

As students decide on their autobiographical events, help them focus on a few important facts so that they can eventually turn their outline into a brief soliloquy. (See the definition of a soliloquy in Learning Objective 2.) Students will perform their autobiographies for the class and can choose to wear any accessories or use props that will support their stories.

As each soliloquy is performed, all of the students in the audience should document at least one similarity and one difference between their own stories and the story being performed.

This lesson is valuable because it is important to practice public speaking and performance in early elementary grades. Many teachers also use readers theater to encourage students to read aloud, in front of peers, and collaborate with others.

Extensions

Use this lesson to encourage self-expression and collaboration in other areas of learning; students can also read aloud stories, poetry, or plays in a class performance. Students can write their own endings to books or create short plays for the class.

The students' autobiographies and soliloquies are wonderful to share with families through a newsletter, book, performance, or video blog.

Assessments

1. Students should write a detailed outline and a shortened version of their autobiographies.

2. Students should turn their outlines into narratives (approximately 1 or 2 minutes long) to perform for the class.

3. As audience members, students should document similarities and differences among their own stories and those of their peers.

A *Hatchet* Soliloquy

Content Areas: Theater, Language Arts

Grade Level: Fifth

Learning Objectives

1. Students will read and summarize the story of *Hatchet* by Gary Paulson.

2. Students will interpret the struggles the protagonist Brian faced and write 2-minute soliloquies based on their interpretations.

3. Students will perform their soliloquies for the class.

Standards

- National Standards for Theater Education 5–8
  - Content Standard 1—Achievement Standard(a)
  - Content Standard 2—Achievement Standard(a)
  - Content Standard 5—Achievement Standard(a)
- National Standards for Elementary Education
  - Standard 1(1.0)
  - Standard 2(2.1)(2.5)
- Common Core State Standards
  - RL.5.1.
  - RL.5.2.
  - W.5.3.
  - SL.5.4.

Procedures

One of the staples of fifth-grade language arts is the book *Hatchet* by Gary Paulson (Aladdin, 1999). The themes in this book include the protagonist's struggles in flying and crashing a plane, learning to survive in the Canadian wilderness by eating whatever food he can find (animals, plants, nuts, and berries), and becoming a craftsman through his creations of a bow and arrow and spears.

After reading the book (and having small group or class discussions), students should interpret Brian's experiences, noting the salient features of the book, the climax, and the ending. Students have to then rewrite the story into a short soliloquy told from Brian's perspective.

Each student should create her or his own version of this, as the narrative document each writes serves both as a text for a performance and as an assessment tool. The performances can be completed in a single class session or spread out over a week. The students in the audience should note how their peers' versions of the story are similar to or different from their own versions.

Extensions

This activity can be applied to any story that is being read by the entire class. If *Hatchet* is not a book that is a part of the curriculum, take a book that has a strong protagonist, and modify this lesson to fit that story. This lesson can also be done in small groups where students adapt the story into a short play.

Assessments

1. Students will read and summarize the story of *Hatchet* by Gary Paulson.

2. Students will interpret the struggles the protagonist Brian faced and write 2-minute soliloquies based on their interpretations.

3. Students will perform their soliloquies and demonstrate appropriate audience behavior.

5

An Introduction to Dance

Kids: they dance before they learn there is anything that isn't music

—William Stafford

The Art of Communication

In its many names and forms, dance embodies the spirit and soul—it is a metaphor for free expression and lack of inhibition. Words that cannot be spoken, thoughts that may be unclear, and stories of timeless generations are communicated through dance.

In a glance at the various cultures of the world, you will find that dance exists within and defines many communities. Folk dances have been used to preserve wisdom and beliefs, to share entertainment and enjoyment, and to communicate the language and ideas of a society. Traditional dancers, in this context, are much like storytellers—with choreographed sequences and specific patterns and beats, and they are adorned in intricate costumes that accentuate the meaning of the story being told.

Studies on children's participation in dance and movement activities have noted the "complex, interactive, and multi-modal" nature of the experience (Bond, 2001, p. 41). Through observations, interviews, and analysis of children's drawings, researchers have examined and interpreted the complexity of dance, describing the interactions between the individual and the social experience (Bond & Richard, 2005; Giguere, 2007; Rajan, 2011).

In a study of third graders' participation in an integrated dance curriculum, Karen Bond and Byron Richard (2005) described students' engagement through kinesthetic social experiences and the development of an aesthetic community. Children's integrated dance experiences foster sensory awareness, spatial focus, personal stylistic preferences, imagination, intellectual engagement, commitment to practice and performance, self-discipline, and form-making abilities (Bond, 2001, p. 41). Similarly, Miriam Giguere (2007) documented 16 fifth graders' creative processes during an integrated dance experience, noting the interactions among peers and how students created and organized movement, described their feelings when dancing, and were aware of their own abilities as good dancers. Through this study, Giguere concluded that dance has an important place in the elementary education curriculum as a way to support cognitive development without being used as a teaching tool for other subject matter.

Performance preparation, and the act of performing itself, has been found to be a motivating component of the dance experience. Elementary students were greatly motivated by their final performance and demonstrated an interest in focusing and working harder through an observable "bond between performance and motivation" (Lazaroff, 2001, p. 28). The collaborative social dynamic of rehearsing and performing created a unique learning environment for students, as their shared dance experiences supported individual and social development.

In the elementary curriculum, dance is also categorized as kinesthetic or movement-based learning (see Pica, 2009). Here, dance is found through simple activities that physically engage children—encouraging them to move their bodies, build focus and balance, and develop an awareness of self and space.

The personal, social, and kinesthetic skills that are fostered through integrated dance activities are summarized in Table 5.1 and serve as a foundation for the examples, vignettes, and lessons presented within this chapter.

Table 5.1	Learning Through Integrated Activities in Dance
Personal Learning	Coordination, Balance, Self-Awareness, Discipline, Focus, Motivation
Social Learning	Cooperation, Collaboration, Awareness of Space
Dance Learning	Self-Expression; Understanding of Patterns, Beats, Sequence, and Rhythms; Choreography, Improvisation

Integrating Dance

The ideas and suggestions for integrating dance into grades K–5 presented here are meant to be starting points for lessons and activities that have the most meaning within your own teaching context and curriculum. Many of the activities look at dance from a broader perspective of kinesthetic and movement-based learning rather than focusing on the development of specific, technical skills.

Dance Autobiography

Reflect on the role of dance in your life—the places and settings within which you dance, have participated in group dances, or have been an audience member for a dance performance.

Use the following prompts to guide your self-reflections:

- My favorite experience with dance is . . .
- My earliest memory with dance is . . .
- My greatest challenge with dance is . . .
- I dance when I am . . .
- My comfort level with dance is . . . because . . .

From these starting points, consider whether you have ever integrated dance (in any form) into your classroom. If you have, why did you choose to do so? Free dance for your students? A celebration of dances around the world? If you have not, why not? Do you think you have two left feet? Feel dancing is best left to professionals?

Recognizing our own experiences, comfort level, strengths, and challenges with dance will strengthen how we integrate dance into the curriculum. Consider all the types of dances you have ever participated in—a sixth-grade school dance, ballroom dancing lessons, free dancing at nightclubs or parties, or dancing alone when no one is around. What is the meaning of dance in your own life, and what is its place in your classroom?

The Process of Integrating Dance

With the absence of physical activity and outlets for free play in our elementary schools and the steady disappearance of recess, there is an even greater need than in the past for providing students with opportunities to move and be active.

Dance in the classroom does not have to be relegated to traditional choreography, specified dance routines, or the building of technical skills. The goal is not to prepare the next professional ballet dancer but to foster elementary students' natural tendency to be energetic and active. Many students turn to afterschool programs that meet the needs for their physical development, such as arts clubs or sports teams. In contrast, the focus within the classroom should be geared toward creative expression, free movement, developing an awareness of self, and a respect for space.

The National Standards for Dance Education note that the basic elements of dance include movement, understanding the relationship between dance and other disciplines, using dance as a means of communication and expression, and identifying various dance styles and the dances of various cultures.

Start with the academic subject area and integrate dance into the lesson. For example, kindergartners can use their bodies to create various letter shapes, while second graders studying estimation can predict how many steps it would take for them to move from one side of the classroom to another. Fifth graders can collaborate to present an interpretive dance on how the ozone layer is affected by our planet and the way we live.

There are many terms used in dance that mirror those in science and math, such as *space, balance, time,* and *energy.* Find ways to draw parallels between these terminologies, so students are aware of the various uses and definitions of these common words.

Building Artistic Vocabulary

Choreography: A specific sequence of dance moves, often created by one individual who is the dance instructor or choreographer

Dynamic Balance: Balance maintained while moving through space, including hopping

Energy: Force used to show intentions

General Space: Shared space in which individuals move and explore

Kinesthetics: Use of the body to learn about physical capabilities, develop body awareness, and gain understanding of the world

Locomotor Skills: Skills that involve movement through space; these include walking, marching, jumping, and skipping

Nonlocomotor Skills: Stationary actions that include stretching, bending, swaying, and shaking

Time: In the context of dance, a term that includes rhythm, speed, emphasis, and duration of a movement

Vignettes and Viewpoints

As you read through these examples, consider the context of each vignette and whether the students are exhibiting dance, movement, or kinesthetic learning. Guide your reflections with the following questions:

- How might I present this activity to my students?
- How do I determine if a student is engaging in a self-initiated movement activity or simply not following directions?
- Is it more important for students to learn specific choreography or to create their own movements?
- How would I assess students' personal, social, and kinesthetic learning?

For a class presentation, third graders are divided into groups of four and instructed to find a creative way to share their researched material. One group of students decides to focus on the water cycle, interpreting the concepts of evaporation, condensation, precipitation, and accumulation through movement of their bodies.

The students are seated in a large circle while the classroom teacher reads a book. The book, Brown Bear, Brown Bear, *by Bill Martin, Jr., and Eric Carle (Henry Holt and Company, 1996), is a favorite of the class, and many students recite aloud parts they have memorized as the teacher reads the story. As the teacher reads, one boy starts fidgeting in his space, tapping his hands on his knees and twisting side to side. The teacher tells him to sit still while she reads, and the boy stops moving briefly before slowly beginning again with a steady pulsing of his hands on his knees.*

The fifth-grade teacher introduces his students to three different styles of instrumental music—waltz, hip hop, and country—and after listening briefly to excerpted selections, asks his students how each selection differs from the others in style, pattern, and context. He further challenges students to decide if they could dance to each style of music, regardless of their preference for or interest in this style.

After lunch, three seven-year-old girls are spinning in a corner of the classroom, raising their arms above their heads, holding hands, then bowing to one another. This pattern continues as they move slowly in a clockwise circle and then continue spinning and twirling. The teacher approaches the girls and states, "That looks lovely! Explain to me what you are doing." One girl responds, "Can't you see— we're prancing ponies!"

Dance Activities for Downtime and Dreaming

While the idea of dance generates images of fast-paced movements and high-energy choreography, some basic elements of dance include focusing the mind, stretching muscles, and controlling the body.

The exercises here are meant for just these purposes—to encourage students to channel their energies through focus and concentration. The goal is to recognize that it takes just as much energy to be still or remain in one position as it does to dance quickly at an upbeat pace. These activities will build your students' awareness of their own bodies, their selves in relation to the others in the classroom, and the space around them.

Stretch and Reach

Engage students in a scenario (picking apples, painting a rainbow, preparing for the Olympics). Begin with a series of simple movements that correspond to the story—taking a step forward and stretching your legs, then alternating with the other leg, reaching arms up and then down in front of you, twisting gently to either side, reaching up and down again. Encourage students to provide suggestions.

Skills—This activity improves focus and clarity as your students concentrate on their own bodies and space. Students are engaged in representing the story being told but are also awakening their own bodies and senses. This works well as a morning or midafternoon activity.

Mirror Me

Pair students with partners and have them face one another. One student (in each pair) should lead the activity, beginning by slowly moving one part of her or his body. The other student should "mirror" the leader. The key to this activity is that the students have to look into each other's eyes, focusing on the other person's expression and using their peripheral vision to imitate and follow the leader.

Skills—This activity fosters focus and concentration through collaboration. Students are engaged in mirroring and imitating one another's movements, and the partner work reinforces the importance of patience and working together. Note—Lucille Ball demonstrates a wonderful example of this activity with Harpo Marx in an episode of *I Love Lucy;* you could choose to share that clip with your students.

Your Own Yoga

Many students are familiar with the concept and idea of yoga poses. There are a variety of poses that are based on animal shapes and postures that appeal to younger children (such as Downward-Facing Dog, Snake, and Cat/Cow), while there are more mature, harder positions for older students (such as Warrior and Twisting Triangle). Present some of these basic yoga poses to your students, but encourage them to create their own poses by naming and describing how their poses focus on one part of the body.

Skills—This activity improves focus and concentration and relieves stress and tension in your students (when practiced on a regular basis). By encouraging students to create their own poses, you are giving them a sense of ownership in this activity. There are multiple text and Internet resources for learning and implementing the basic yoga poses described here.

Lessons and Assessments

Dance is commonly found in early childhood (as opposed to upper elementary) settings with movement and physical activities that are seamlessly integrated into free play and group activities. This section includes 16 examples of integrated dance lessons. Although there are specific lessons targeted toward each grade level, I encourage you to read through all the lessons, to draw upon and modify any activities that are relevant to your own setting.

For each lesson presented in the following section, I have included learning objectives, standards for dance education, standards for early childhood and elementary education, specific procedures for implementing the lesson, extensions to the activity, and applicable instruments for assessing learning. The arts standards integrated into each lesson are adopted from the National Standards for Dance Education. Each lesson is connected to the relevant core standards for early childhood education and elementary education and to the Common Core standards for math and language arts.

Remember that the terms *dance* and *movement* are used almost interchangeably, in that these activities are about self-expression with the body and moving in ways that are comfortable, rather than about teaching rigid, choreographed sequences. As always, by inviting students to share their own ideas and definitions, the lessons maintain a student-centered approach, a philosophy that is central to integrated arts activities.

Estimate Me

Content Areas: Dance, Math

Grade Level: Second

Learning Objectives

1. Students will estimate how many steps it will take to get from one side of the classroom to the other side.

2. Students will create different ways to move across the classroom.

Standards

- National Standards for Dance Education K–4
  - o Content Standard 1—Achievement Standards(a)(b)
  - o Content Standard 4—Achievement Standard(a)
- National Standards for Early Childhood Education
  - o Standard 4(c)
  - o Standard 5(c)
- Common Core State Standards
  - o 2.MD.1.
  - o 2.MD.2.
  - o 2.MD.3.

Procedures

Gather students as a group, and explain (or review) the concept of estimation. Tell students they will be estimating how many steps it will take to move from one side of the classroom to another. Students should estimate of the total number of steps each child in the class will take and write their individual estimations in a journal or on a worksheet.

After they have written their estimations, students should move from one side of the class to the other individually (or two at a time), counting their steps. This activity should then be extended as students choose different methods by which to move across the classroom. Make some suggestions, or ask students to provide ideas. Some examples might be crawling, jumping, hopping, and skipping.

While the focus of this lesson is on building capacities for estimating, the process should be through students' physical movement and use of their bodies.

Extensions

Take the concept of estimating with movement into a variety of different settings, such as hallways, the cafeteria, the playground, and outdoors. To build on these skills, encourage students to estimate different spaces in their homes and community and share their results with the class.

Assessments

1. Students should document their estimations on a worksheet or in a journal. This first objective can also be shared verbally and documented for the entire class.

2. Students should contribute different ways of moving across the classroom and estimate the number of "steps" for each, making note of their ideas and results.

Identical Shapes

Content Areas: Dance, Math

Grade Level: Third

Learning Objectives

1. Students will create various geometric shapes using their bodies.

2. Students will imitate the shapes made by their partners or individuals in their small groups.

Standards

- National Standards for Dance Education K–4
  - Content Standard 1—Achievement Standards(c)(d)
  - Content Standard 2—Achievement Standards(c)(d)
- National Standards for Early Childhood Education
  - Standard 1(a)
  - Standard 3(c)
  - Standard 4(c)
- Common Core State Standards
  - 3.G.1.

Procedures

Students will use their bodies to create geometric shapes by recognizing the number of sides and elements of the shape. The shapes can be as simple as a circle or more complicated, such as a pentagon or octagon. The goal is for students to recognize that they need to use their bodies to represent characteristics of the shape (such as five angles or five sides) as opposed to an exact physical representation.

Students can be paired up or work in a small group. Each student should document which shapes they chose to create with their bodies, which shapes they imitated, and the characteristics of each shape on their lists.

Extensions

This activity can be extended by including the use of props, chairs, tables, or any smaller handheld accessories to help students create more complicated shapes. While this is inherently a movement-based activity, additional goals include encouraging focus among partners (a theater skill) and recognition of geometric shapes (a math skill).

Assessments

1. Students should create at least two different shapes with their bodies, recognizing verbally and in writing what the components and angles are that make up each shape.

2. Students should work collaboratively with a partner or in a small group to imitate and recognize shapes.

Awkward Angles

Content Areas: Dance, Math

Grade Level: Fourth

Learning Objectives

1. Students will identify the characteristics of acute, obtuse, straight, and right angles.

2. Students will interpret the shape of each angle with their bodies.

Standards

- National Standards for Dance Education K–4
  - Content Standard 1—Achievement Standard(c)
  - Content Standard 2—Achievement Standard(b)
- National Standards for Elementary Education
  - Standard 2(2.3)(2.5)
  - Standard 3(3.5)
  - Standard 4(4.0)
- Common Core State Standards
  - 4.G.1.
  - 4.G.2.

Procedures

Explain to students that they will use their bodies to move into positions that represent various angles. Students should first write down specific angles and their characteristics, noting similarities and differences among angles. In pairs (or small groups), students should use their bodies to create an angle, and the degrees should be checked or measured by a peer. This is a practice session for the actual activity.

Divide the class in half. You (or someone you select as the leader) will call out an angle and one person on each team has to shape his or her body into that angle. The person that makes the angle the fastest and that represents it most accurately wins one point. The team with the most points wins.

Encourage students to be creative with this activity! It is not often fourth graders get a chance to move and use their bodies in a way that connects with math. The goal here is to try to create different angles, work collaboratively with peers to measure and document which angles they created, and note how they used their bodies to create an angle. Perhaps also play some music in the background, anything instrumental and upbeat to foster a playful environment for this activity.

Extensions

Try to encourage students to create more complicated angles with their bodies, use props, and measure angles around the classroom.

Assessments

1. Students should write down the degrees of each angle and characteristics of each angle.

2. For each angle they created, students should document how they used their bodies, noting why they chose to move as they did.

Dance Sequence

Content Areas: Dance, Math

Grade Level: Fifth

Learning Objectives

1. Students will identify the simple and common patterns that compose various dances.

2. Students will work in small groups to choreograph a dance that conforms to one of the patterns.

3. Students will perform their dance for the class or a larger audience.

Standards

- National Standards for Dance Education 5–8
  - Content Standard 1—Achievement Standards(a)(b)(c)
  - Content Standard 2—Achievement Standards(a)(b)
- National Standards for Elementary Education
  - Standard 1(1.0)
  - Standard 2(2.3)(2.5)
  - Standard 3(3.5)
- Common Core State Standards
  - 5.OA.3.

Procedures

Dance sequences are composed of simple and complex patterns. When written down, these patterns are represented by letters. The patterns use a specific style and sequence in association with each letter. Here are some common patterns used in dances: ABA, ABC, ABABA, ABB, AAB, AABA.

Let us take the ABA pattern as an example. If the movements in A require fast turns and quick steps, the movements in B might be slower, simpler, and more calming. Then, when A returns, the fast turns and quick steps return. If possible, assign one or two students to create the dance steps for each letter in the pattern.

Students should become familiar with the various patterns, recognizing the association between the letters and movements or music. Place students in groups of three or four and have each group select a pattern for which they will choreograph a dance. Each group will perform their dance for the class, and the students who are in the audience have to determine which pattern was used.

Extensions

Since the focus of this lesson is on patterns and sequencing, encourage students to try even more complex movements. The dances do not need to be long, but they need to be specific in which movements are associated with each letter in the pattern and sequence.

Assessments

1. Students should verbally describe the patterns and sequences associated with dance and the relationship between the letters and movements.

2. Students should actively participate and contribute to movements in the group dance.

3. Students should participate in the performance and act as supportive audience members.

Don't Erupt on Me!

Content Areas: Dance, Science

Grade Level: Second

Learning Objectives

1. Students will identify and describe the process of a volcanic eruption.

2. Students will interpret the eruption process from lava within the volcano to the final eruption and smoke.

Standards

- National Standards for Dance Education K–4
  - Content Standard 1—Achievement Standard(a)
  - Content Standard 2—Achievement Standards(a)(b)
  - Content Standard 7—Achievement Standard(a)
- National Standards for Early Childhood Education
  - Standard 1(a)
  - Standard 4(c)
  - Standard 5(c)

Procedures

This lesson can take place at any point in time as students are learning about volcanoes—either at the beginning or near the end as a culminating activity. Students should identify the steps of a volcanic eruption—from the compression of gas to an eruption. Some vocabulary words to focus on include *molten lava, magma, eruption, steam,* and *gas.* More challenging concepts include *magmatic eruptions, phreato-magmatic eruptions,* and *phreatic eruptions.*

Once students recognize the basic characteristics of each eruption, divide them into groups to choreograph their own creative movements. Each group should make sure to demonstrate the specific steps of the eruption process and should be encouraged to use props, music, or sounds to emphasize their choreography.

Extensions

Turning a scientific process into creative movement is a great way to physically involve students in a lesson. Some other ideas include having students interpret the water cycle, the cycle of seeds, the butterfly life cycle, and the growth of a tree.

Assessments

1. Students should be able to describe different volcanic eruptions and the process of a volcanic eruption both verbally and in written work.

2. In their groups, each student should contribute to the creative movement process, selecting movements that are associated with the different stages of an eruption and performing the collective movements for the class.

Crazy Clouds

Content Areas: Dance, Science

Grade Level: Third

Learning Objectives

1. Students will observe the pattern of clouds outside (over the course of a day or week).

2. Students will move and interpret the pattern of clouds with their bodies based on changes in the weather and wind.

Standards

- National Standards for Dance Education K–4
  - Content Standard 1—Achievement Standard(a)
  - Content Standard 2—Achievement Standards(a)(b)
  - Content Standard 7—Achievement Standard(a)
- National Standards for Early Childhood Education
  - Standard 1(a)
  - Standard 3(c)
  - Standard 4(b)

Procedures

The ideal preparation for this lesson is having students observe and document cloud patterns and movements over the course of one week. Each day, students should look outside, observe, and describe the shapes and patterns they see in the clouds. Students should document the other weather conditions that might affect the clouds' movements, including sunshine or winds.

After one week, students should gather their notes and summarize their observations. Gather the students as a large group and discuss each student's observations—what changes did they observe in the clouds? How did the clouds move? What directions where the clouds moving?

Students should then interpret the movements of the clouds using their bodies. Place students into small groups of three or four and assign them one weather condition associated with a certain type of cloud. Some cloud types include *cirrus, altrostratus, stratocumulus, nimbostratus,* and *cumulonimbus.*

Extensions

This activity could be easily extended to a longer period of time, having students track cloud movements for a month or at different locations (such as at home and at school).

Assessments

1. Each student should individually document her or his observations of clouds in a journal.

2. The teacher should complete a Crazy Clouds Student Checklist for each student.

Crazy Clouds Student Checklist

Actively participated in the small group creative dance	Yes	No
Provided at least one suggestion for the group	Yes	No
Demonstrated balance of body when moving	Yes	No
Demonstrated use of gross motor skills	Yes	No

Notes:

Planet Power

Content Areas: Dance, Science

Grade Level: Fourth

Learning Objectives

1. Students will improvise movements based on characteristics of the planets. For example, spinning is a characteristic that could be associated with the rings of Saturn, and red and fiery are characteristics associated with Mars.

2. Students will contribute suggestions for representing the various characteristics in movement and participate in a group dance.

Standards

- National Standards for Dance Education K–4
  - o Content Standard 2—Achievement Standards(a)(b)
  - o Content Standard 3—Achievement Standard(b)
  - o Content Standard 7—Achievement Standard(a)
- National Standards for Elementary Education
  - o Standard 2(2.2)(2.5)
  - o Standard 3(3.5)

Procedures

By fourth grade, planets and the solar system are a strong part of students' knowledge base in science. This lesson builds upon the characteristics of the planets by engaging students in creative movement.

Have students brainstorm characteristics, descriptive words, and ideas that they associate most with each of the planets. In small groups or as a class, students should share their ideas and be given the opportunity to explore movements that they feel best represent their interpretations of the words on their brainstorming list.

Once students have had a chance to explore and create movements, place students into small groups, and assign each group a planet for which they will create a choreographed and improvised dance. Each student in the group must contribute movements, and the dance should be a creative story of the planet's characteristics. The dance must also include choreographed moves (that the students all created and practiced together) and time for individual improvisation (on-the-spot dancing).

The students who compose the audience as each group dances should try to determine which planet is being shown in the performance, and specifically what specific words or characteristics are associated with the movements they observe.

Extensions

The idea for this lesson is to go beyond literal interpretations of movements and feelings (which is the primary focus in early elementary grades). Rather, students should find new ways of expressing the words and concepts—for example, if Mars is red, how would students use their bodies to interpret red? How does red feel? How does Mars act? This moves the activity beyond basic movements to more complex, creative thinking.

This lesson can include other dimensions of the solar system or be adapted to focus on any range of topics that allow students to create movements for specific descriptions.

Assessments

1. Students should improvise and create their own interpretations prior to finalizing a group dance.

2. The dance can be assessed with the Planet Power Rubric.

Planet Power Rubric			
Grading Criteria	*1*	*2*	*3*
Interpretation	Student moved around the room in the group dance.	Student interpreted different characteristics of the planets with the body.	Student used the body in new ways while interpreting the planets.
Contribution	Student contributed at least one movement idea to the group dance.	Student contributed two movement ideas to the group dance.	Student demonstrated leadership in the group dance.
Participation	Student participated minimally as required but did not go beyond the basic elements of movement.	Student actively participated and demonstrated some new ideas in use of words and body movements.	Student demonstrated creativity and innovation with words and use of body movements when dancing.

No Zone Ozone

Content Areas: Dance, Science

Grade Level: Fifth

Learning Objectives

1. Students will use gestures and movements to present an interpretive story on how the layer of ozone around our planet is affected by human activity.

2. Students will work in groups of three to create and perform their story.

Standards

- National Standards for Dance Education 5–8
  - Content Standard 2—Achievement Standards(b)(c)
  - Content Standard 3—Achievement Standards(a)(b)
- National Standards for Elementary Education
  - Standard 2(2.2)(2.5)
  - Standard 3(3.5)

Procedures

The destruction of the ozone layer is a relevant and interesting topic for students, particularly when they are considering how they can help save and protect our planet. Engage students in a discussion of the ozone layer, the components of the ozone, and the changes that are taking place. Why is the ozone layer deteriorating? What are the causes and concerns? What can we do to enact change?

In groups of three, students should discuss and create a short narrative telling the story of the ozone layer. The story should include the characteristics of the ozone, why we need the ozone, and how the ozone is affected by our planet and our lifestyles.

Each group needs to then translate their written narrative into a creative movement piece, where each group member will contribute ideas for gestures and movements that will accurately portray their story. The students may not use any words but may use sounds, beats, or rhythms with their bodies, gestures, and hand motions to emphasize words or ideas.

Extensions

If possible, students should perform their pieces (and even explore the process) outside rather than indoors to get a full understanding of the connections between the planet, weather, and our individual choices in life. Filming or performing these pieces for a larger audience would be a wonderful way for students to share their creativity and ideas.

Assessments

1. Each student should contribute at least one idea for the story, perhaps being responsible for the beginning, middle, or end of the sequence.

2. All students should actively participate, engaging in gestures, movements, and collaboration with their peers as they communicate their story.

Growing Like a Seed

Content Areas: Dance, Social Studies, Science

Grade Level: Kindergarten

Learning Objectives

1. Students will identify the stages of a seed's growth and recognize how seeds travel around the world.

2. Students will use their bodies to represent the growth of a seed into a plant.

Standards

- National Standards for Dance Education K–4
  - Content Standard 2—Achievement Standard(a)
  - Content Standard 3—Achievement Standard(a)
  - Content Standard 7—Achievement Standard(a)
- National Standards for Early Childhood Education
  - Standard 1(a)(b)
  - Standard 5(c)

Procedures

Begin the lesson by showing students a variety of seeds, such as pumpkin, sunflower, apple, hibiscus, watermelon, and marigold seeds. Have students examine the seeds, noting the colors, textures, and sizes of the various seeds, and ask them questions about what they notice—how the seeds feel and look.

Explain to students that seeds are planted in the ground or soil and become something much larger—they grow! If possible, bring images or actual materials to show students how the seeds start and then eventually become a flower or fruit.

As students continue to learn about how seeds are planted and watered, need sunshine and care, and eventually sprout and grow, engage students in a movement activity where they use their bodies to act as the seeds. Ask students to outline the steps—what comes first, second, third? Ask students how *they* would act as a seed being placed in the soil, being buried, and then sprouting. Use their suggestions to build this movement activity.

Explore where seeds travel from one location to another, carried by the wind and sprouting where they settle down. Have students imagine that they are seeds that are traveling somewhere far away—what type of seeds would they be, and where would they go?

Extensions

An extension of this lesson is to have each student select a flower seed from a pile and grow her or his own flower over the course of time.

Assessments

1. Students should verbally describe the stages of a seed's growth, and complete the Growing Like a Seed Worksheet by putting either pictures of the plant at different stages of growth or actual materials from it (such as seeds, soil, leaves, and flowers) in chronological order in each of the six boxes (that is, the seed in Box 1, the sprout in Box 2, the seedling in Box 3, etc.). The written section is optional and can be completed by the classroom teacher with the student's response.

2. Students should use their bodies to fully participate in the creative movement activity.

Growing Like a Seed	
1.	2.
3.	4.
5.	6.

(OPTIONAL) If I were a seed, I would be a _____

I would travel to _____

_____

Butterfly Life Cycle

Content Areas: Dance, Social Studies, Science

Grade Level: First

Learning Objectives

1. Students will identify each of the steps in the butterfly's life cycle and compare butterflies of different geographic regions.

2. Students will act out the stages of the butterfly's life cycle.

Standards

- National Standards for Dance Education K–4
  - Content Standard 1—Achievement Standard(a)
  - Content Standard 2—Achievement Standard(a)
  - Content Standard 3—Achievement Standard(a)
- National Standards for Early Childhood Education
  - Standard 1(a)(b)
  - Standard 4(c)
  - Standard 5(c)

Procedures

Acting out the life cycle of the butterfly is a popular way to engage young students. The key to this lesson is to give the students ownership over their movements rather than requiring everyone to move the same way. Ask students to interpret a butterfly's movements as it grows from its cocoon into a final, beautiful butterfly.

Engage students through questions on what it feels like to be in the cocoon, to get bigger, and to burst open to be a butterfly. How is crawling like a caterpillar different from flying in the air? What are the strengths and challenges of each situation? How does the caterpillar survive in a way that is different from the way a butterfly survives?

As students continue to build on these ideas, ensure that they recognize the stages of a butterfly's life cycle (either through verbal questioning or through review of their written work), and use class discussions to ask students where they would live as a butterfly, why they would choose to live in that geographic region, and how their appearance (colors, size) would be affected by this choice. Here are some examples of choices they could make:

The monarch butterfly migrates for long distances.

The painted lady (or cosmopolitan) butterfly is found in nearly every geographic region.

During the monsoons in India, butterflies have a long period of time to migrate.

Danaini (or milkweed) butterflies are prominent in Asia and Africa.

Extensions

There are a variety of visual art activities that can be used with students to make representations of their ideas about butterflies. If possible, having students examine and interact with real butterflies prior to this lesson will help them to formulate their own ideas of the butterfly life cycle and movements, or this can serve as a wonderful culmination of this creative movement activity.

Assessments

1. Each student should identify the stages of the butterfly's life cycle. If possible, they should also be able to describe how specific butterflies are associated with different geographic regions.

2. Either as a class or in small groups, students should interpret the butterfly's life cycle by using their bodies to tell their story.

Chinese New Year

Content Areas: Dance, Social Studies, Language Arts

Grade Level: Second

Learning Objectives

1. Students will identify the purpose and role of the dragon in the Chinese New Year.

2. Students will create movements as a class to imitate a Chinese dragon in a New Year parade.

3. Students will create their own story for the dragon.

Standards

- National Standards for Dance Education K–4
  - Content Standard 1—Achievement Standard(a)
  - Content Standard 2—Achievement Standard(a)
  - Content Standard 5—Achievement Standard(a)
- National Standards for Early Childhood Education
  - Standard 4(c)
  - Standard 5(c)

Procedures

The Chinese New Year is a wonderful festival filled with stories, traditions, brilliant colors, music, and food. Beginning this lesson with a book or presentation is a simple way to engage students in the basic traditions of the Chinese New Year and in understanding the role and significance of the dragon.

Ask students how they would describe images of the dragon (based on pictures you might share or images that students bring into class): What colors and patterns do they notice? Why do they think the dragon is an important symbol? What other symbol or animal might they choose instead?

If possible, students should watch an actual procession of the dragon in a Chinese New Year parade. There are also some wonderful toys that show the fluidity and movements of the dragon's body. Have the students collaborate to create their own dragon dance. What movements did they choose? How do they have to work together? What is each person's role in shaping and moving the dragon?

As a culmination of this group creative movement activity, each student should write a story for the dragon, describing the dragon's personality and preferences, place in the history of China, and contributions to the parade and New Year celebration.

Extensions

Clearly, this is a lesson that should be implemented around February, when the Chinese New Year begins, but the idea can be modified by focusing on a symbol of another celebration. Some other festivals on which students could focus include Diwali (India), Oktoberfest (Germany), Mardi Gras (United States), and Ch'ing Ming (China).

Assessments

1. Students should verbally identify the dragon's role and purpose in the Chinese New Year.

2. Each student should contribute at least one idea to the group creative movement as a dragon.

3. In a journal or on a separate sheet of paper, each student should write a story about the dragon and reflect on her or his collaborative role within the group. This could also be a verbal presentation.

How Does a Giraffe Dance?

Content Areas: Dance, Music, Social Studies, Language Arts

Grade Level: Third

Learning Objectives

1. Students will differentiate between four different genres of music: waltz, rock and roll, tango, and cha-cha-cha.

2. Students will interpret each genre of music through a group dance.

3. Students will identify the types of movement they associate with each type of music and recognize the music's country of origination.

Standards

- National Standards for Dance Education K–4
  - o Content Standard 2—Achievement Standard(a)
  - o Content Standard 5—Achievement Standard(a)
- National Standards for Early Childhood Education
  - o Standard 1(a)(b)
  - o Standard 5(c)

Procedures

Begin by reading the book (or engaging students in a group read, based on their reading levels) *Giraffes Can't Dance* by Giles Andreae and Guy Parker-Rees (Orchard Books, 2001). This book is intended for children ages four to eight, so encourage your students to read this independently. If you read the story aloud, ask students about the characteristics of each genre of music, and create a list of words they use to describe each genre through sounds, colors, textures, or imagery in the pictures in the book.

Explain how the waltz originated in Austria through compositions such as The Blue Danube by Johann Strauss, Jr. There were specific, three-part movements associated with the waltz, and people would dance in large, choreographed groups.

Rock and roll was famous in America, and Elvis Presley in the 1950s and the Beatles in the 1960s are some of the most recognized musicians associated with this type of music.

The tango is a passionate dance between a man and a woman and originated in Argentina. Very often the woman is depicted wearing a striking red dress and holding a rose in her mouth, and the man is dressed in a black suit. Dancers during the tango are very fierce and sharp, as their movements are timed exactly with the fast rhythms of the music.

The cha-cha-cha is a lively, upbeat dance that originated in Cuba. The music is fast and often made up of various rhythms and patterns.

In a large group discussion, categorize specific characteristics of each dance style and ask students what they think the music sounds like (referencing words and ideas from the book). Ask how they might move to rock and roll versus the cha-cha-cha. What would they do differently with their bodies?

Students should have some time then to explore the different musical styles. Play selections of music for students to listen to, and encourage them to move freely, taking time to discuss afterwards what choices they made, how the music felt, and how they would describe the movements to someone else. Continue to draw connections between the music and dance styles and their countries of origin.

Extensions

This lesson is a great starting point for discussing genres of music and dance, and how music and dance are often connected in a very strong way. Ask students what types of music they listen to at home or if they dance at home. Introduce line dancing, jitterbugging, or the fox-trot—all traditional dance styles. Many of the reality shows on television showcase ballroom dancing and various other dance styles, and these might be another platform from which to generate discussions about movement, music, and the countries associated with particular dance styles.

Assessments

1. Students should be able to distinguish among musical styles when they hear the music played and should be able to provide descriptive words for each style.

2. Students should actively participate in the group dances.

3. Students should relate specific dance styles to their countries of origin.

Letter Bodies

Content Areas: Dance, Language Arts

Grade Level: Kindergarten

Learning Objectives

1. Students will use their bodies to create letters in the alphabet.

2. Students will spell their names using their bodies.

Standards

- National Standards for Dance Education K–4
  - Content Standard 1—Achievement Standards(a)(b)
  - Content Standard 3—Achievement Standard(b)
- National Standards for Early Childhood Education
  - Standard 1(a)
  - Standard 3(c)
- Common Core State Standards
  - SL.K.6.
  - L.K.1.
  - L.K.2.

Procedures

As students continue to recognize different letters and characteristics unique to each letter, engage students by asking them to all create the letter *A* using their bodies. Ask them how they might do this: What parts of their body will they use? How does the letter *A* look?

Begin this activity in a large group with all students in the class participating and exploring the shapes of each letter with their bodies. As students begin to recognize the letters, continue through the alphabet, or focus on the letters of each student's name.

Students should continue to practice this activity even when they start learning to write so that they build upon and reinforce their understanding of the shapes and lines that they created using their own bodies. This process will assist them with transferring those ideas onto paper.

Extensions

Build this activity based on each student's skill level. If students are able to recognize only the first letter of their names, then that is a great place to start. For students who are more advanced, ask them to spell their peers' names or names of parents or siblings.

Assessments

1. Observe students' participation as a class by calling out a letter and identifying which students recognize the shape of the letter and use their bodies to create the shape.

2. Students should be able to use their bodies to represent the first letters of their names, or each student should spell her or his entire name individually.

Carnival of the Animals

Content Areas: Dance, Language Arts, Science

Grade Level: First

Learning Objectives

1. Students will create movements to represent the animals in the book *Carnival of the Animals.*

2. Students will demonstrate their movements while listening to various musical selections associated with animals.

3. Students will describe their movement choices in correlation to each animal.

Standards

- National Standards for Dance Education K–4
  - o Content Standard 1—Achievement Standards(a)(b)
  - o Content Standard 2—Achievement Standards(a)(b)
  - o Content Standard 3—Achievement Standard(b)
- National Standards for Early Childhood Education
  - o Standard 1(a)
  - o Standard 3(c)
  - o Standard 4(c)
- Common Core State Standards
  - o RL.1.1.
  - o RL.1.3.
  - o RI.1.4.
  - o SL.1.1.

Procedures

Begin by reading the book, *Carnival of the Animals: Classical Music for Kids,* by Camille Saint-Saens (composer of the music), Barrie C. Turner (author), and Sue Williams (illustrator) (Henry Holt and Company, 1999). This book is a wonderful resource that comes with a compilation of music from Saint-Saens' compositions, aligning his music about different animals with vivid, bright imagery and text.

Ask students how they believe the animals move; importantly, their responses need not conform to the typical responses (such as "a kangaroo hops"). Create a list of the descriptive words that students contribute to the discussion, and then play the music that is associated with each animal. Build upon the previous discussion by asking students what they hear, what movements they hear in the music, and which animal they think of when they listen to the music.

As you continue playing the music (or a few selections), engage students in creative movement by encouraging them to move as they feel, based on what they hear in the music, and as whatever animal comes to mind. Note the students who are creating their own movements and the individual and group choices students make.

As a final discussion, ask each student what movements they created with the music and how their own movements related to the animals referenced in the music.

Extensions

A wonderful extension to this is to go beyond the animals listed in the book and ask students to find different animals, describe their characteristics or observe their movements, and create movements representative of each animal.

Assessments

1. Teachers can use the Carnival of the Animals Checklist to note each student's participation in the activity.

Carnival of the Animals Checklist

Student contributed a movement for each animal in the group dance.	Yes	No
Student actively participated in the group dance.	Yes	No
Student described individual choices for movements for each animal.	Yes	No

Notes:

Spring Is Here

Content Areas: Dance, Language Arts, Science

Grade Level: Second

Learning Objectives

1. Students will identify the characteristics of spring after reading various poems.

2. Students will create movements that correlate with their suggested characteristics of spring.

3. Students will express the characteristics of spring in a group dance using ribbon sticks, scarves, or free expression with their bodies.

Standards

- National Standards for Dance Education K–4
    - Content Standard 3—Achievement Standard(b)
    - Content Standard 4—Achievement Standard(a)
- National Standards for Early Childhood Education
    - Standard 1(a)
    - Standard 4(a)(b)
- Common Core State Standards
    - RL.2.4.
    - RI.2.4.
    - RI.2.6.
    - RI.2.7.
    - SL.2.5.

Procedures

As a class or with students in small groups, read through a variety of poems that describe the season of spring. Ask students what are descriptive words that they notice, how do the words relate to spring, and what do the poems make them think of and feel?

Students should create their own lists of specific characteristics from each poem and movements that they associate with the words.

For example, in Matsuo Basho's poem, "Spring Rain," how might a student move or act as spring rain leaking through the roof?

In groups of three or four, students should create movements that represent the words and ideas presented in a poem about spring. Each student should contribute one idea to the movement piece, and students can decide whether they want to use any accessories (such as scarves or ribbons) during their performance. Each group should perform their piece for the class while another student (or the teacher) reads the poem aloud.

Some suggested poems include the following: "Spring Rain," by Matsuo Basho; "Singing," by Robert Louis Stevenson; and "A Child of Spring," by Ellen Robena Field.

Extensions

This activity can be used for any season, place, or event, as the goal is for students to identify descriptive words and create movements to represent them. Essentially, students are telling a story or enacting the poem with their bodies and movements. A key aspect of this lesson is to have the poem read aloud as students perform, ensuring that their movements are coordinated with specific words and ideas.

Assessments

1. Students create a list of specific characteristics and descriptive words from a poem about spring.

2. Students have a list of correlating movements for each of the characteristics they have listed.

3. Students participate in the creation and performance of a group dance related to their assigned poem.

Water, Water, Everywhere

Content Areas: Dance, Language Arts, Science

Grade Level: Third

Learning Objectives

1. Students will identify the various components of the water cycle and create a story about it.

2. Students will work in pairs or small groups to create movements corresponding to their story of the water cycle.

Standards

- National Standards for Dance Education K–4
  - Content Standard 1(a)
  - Content Standard 3(b)
- National Standards for Early Childhood Education
  - Standard 4(c)
  - Standard 5(b)
- Common Core State Standards
  - RI.3.3.
  - W.3.3.

Procedures

As students are learning about the water cycle, ensure that each student can identify the major components of the cycle—from ground water flow to evaporation to precipitation and percolation.

In small groups, students should brainstorm ideas for a story about the water cycle. Who should be in the story? What parts will each person play? Are they acting as people, land, or water? How is the water cycle impacted by people? Students should write a short narrative of their collective story and create movements for the story, interpreting their ideas in a dance.

Students should then practice their dance, ensuring that their movements tell the story in their narrative. Encourage students to move around the classroom, use their entire bodies, and use props and sounds to tell their story effectively.

Extensions

Students can build on this activity to enact more than just the water cycle; in more complex narratives, they could enact the relationship between their lifestyles and the water cycle, the connection between the water cycle and the rainforest, or the impact of animals and plant life on the water cycle.

Assessments

1. Students should individually list the components of the water cycle in a journal or on a worksheet. This list will form the foundation of the story students will create within their small groups.

2. Each student should actively participate in the group creative movement and provide suggestions for interpreting the story.

6

An Introduction to Musical Theater

The hills are alive with the sound of music.

—Maria in *The Sound of Music*

From Broadway to Backpacks

Musical theater is a culmination of the performing arts. Begin with a touching script; add dramatic music, memorable songs, and perfectly synchronized choreography coupled with fantastic costumes, complex sets, and bright lights, and you have a classic musical theater production.

The musical is an inherently American performing art form, tracing its roots from the performers of vaudeville in the 1920s to the movie musicals of the late 1930s and 1940s (Kislan, 1980). Some of the most famous actors and actresses in American history began in movie musicals; in fact, the ability to sing and/or dance was often a requirement to be a film actor.

Through the global influences of popular composers and librettists such as Rodgers and Hammerstein and George and Ira Gershwin, musical theater found a niche in Europe and Asia, where markets for touring productions and school-based musical theater began to develop. Although musical theater found its beginnings with stories of unrequited love, the turbulent times of 1950s and 1960s brought with them musicals based on strong social and political messages of war, despair, and depression (Kislan, 1980). During this time, the musical remained as a form of entertainment but now carried with it strong ties to community issues for the producers and audience members.

Definitions of musical theater have evolved through time from simple productions to grand spectacles, follies, and musical revues. The terms *musical, show,* and *production* are often used synonymously with musical theater. Parallel to musical theater, operas and operettas also include elements of music, theater, and dance. Many educators and artists view musical theater as based in theater, and operas and operettas as based in music. Arguably, each carries with it elements of the performing arts, and so these discussions are often rooted in distinctions of ownership of these genres in teaching and research.

While many major cities across the world currently have theater districts or famous performance venues for musical theater, Broadway remains the location of the pinnacle of this art form. Finding a place on Broadway is the goal for nearly every performer and producer—a validation of self and show through the garnered respect of critics and audiences alike. With a resurgence of interest in musical theater in the early 1990s, producers, composers, and educators collaborated to create musicals that were age appropriate for younger audiences and performers and imparted a specific message or theme. Some of these musicals require licensing to be produced, while others are more easily integrated into the classroom with fully orchestrated recordings and ideas for costumes and choreography that may be freely copied from the original productions.

The success of movies such as Disney's *High School Musical* and the television show *Glee,* and the remakes of popular musicals with younger actors (such as *Footloose*), demonstrate how musical theater has found a renowned place in popular culture, one that targets younger audiences and performers.

Musical theater has profound effects on its performers and is particularly transformative for children (Rajan, 2009, in press). Through participation in musical theater in school-based, community, and professional settings, children augment self-confidence and pride while battling with insecurities and doubt of their own abilities. The process of rehearsing and preparing for a show also creates a sense of community as children build friendships and turn to their peers for support and comfort when performing on stage. For both the amateur and professional performer, developing artistic skills as a singer, actor, or dancer is a recognized, necessary step in becoming a performing artist.

The personal, social, and artistic skills that are fostered through integrated musical theater activities are summarized in Table 6.1 and blend many of the capacities represented through participation in music, theater, and dance.

Table 6.1	Learning Through Integrated Activities in Musical Theater
Personal Learning	Motivation, Focus, Individual Artistic Skills (in Music, Theater, Dance), Developing a Character, Self-Confidence, Commitment, Professionalism
Social Learning	Collaboration, Support, Teamwork, Ensemble
Artistic Learning	Performance, Being on Stage, Utilizing Costumes and Makeup, Interacting With Props and Scenery, Technical Aspects of Production

Integrating Musical Theater

The ideas and suggestions for integrating musicals into grades K–5 presented here are meant to engage both you and your students in the study of musical theater. The shows included in this section are representative of Broadway and Off-Broadway musicals. While some of the musicals and songs may be familiar to you, others will be new. I encourage you to use these ideas as starting points—they can form the foundation and focus of a lesson as you use different musicals, scripts, and songs interchangeably.

Musical Theater Autobiography

When you think of musical theater, what is the first thing that comes to mind? Reflect here on the role of musical theater in your life—consider your definition of and associations with this art form, your favorite and least favorite songs, your comfort and challenges with musicals.

Use the following prompts to guide your self-reflections:

- Musical theater is . . .
- My favorite musical is . . .
- My greatest challenge with musical theater is . . .
- I was introduced to musical theater . . .

From these starting points, consider whether you have ever integrated musical theater into your classroom. If you have, what was the activity? A favorite song to start the day? Taking your students to a live show? If you have not, why not? Not familiar with musicals? Unsure how to integrate musical theater?

Since musical theater is not as commonly used in classrooms as music, theater, and dance, it is important to have a strong grasp of this art form, an understanding of why musical theater is important, and an awareness of how it should be used to teach specific concepts and lessons.

The Process of Integrating Musical Theater

Musical theater teaches more than just the performing arts. The history of this art form brings with it strong personal and societal messages: responses to war, despair, and depression, and examples of friendships, families, culture, and unrequited love.

Unlike the other performing art forms, which have specific standards with which to align, musical theater is an all encompassing genre, with elements of music, theater, *and* dance. When integrating musical theater, then, it is important to first consider which of these three elements is the focus of the lesson, building from there to align with specific arts and content area standards.

Begin always with the academic content area that is important to the lesson. (Sometimes, if you have a particular musical, scene, song, or dance in mind, you can identify the themes and build the lesson from there.) Consider how kindergartners can study rainbows after listening to the song "Over the Rainbow" from *The Wizard of Oz;* first graders can estimate, sort, and categorize the felines in the show *Cats;* fourth graders can study ecosystems after watching *The Lion King;* and fifth graders can explore the generations within their own family after listening to "Chop Suey" from *Flower Drum Song.*

Musical theater also has a unique terminology, much of which refers to the specific aspects of rehearsals and performance, but some of which also draws upon vocabulary in music, theater, and dance. With that in mind, use these words as an opportunity to build on the vocabulary presented throughout this book, drawing connections between disciplines and helping students find meaning through their participation in musical theater activities.

Building Artistic Vocabulary

Auditions: The process of casting for a show, often requiring performers to read from the script, sing a prepared musical selection, and learn a choreographed dance sequence

Callbacks: The final round of auditions where individual performers are selected for additional acting, singing, or dancing before the cast list is determined

Costumes: The outfits that performers wear during their performances—some are simple, while others can be quite elaborate and require hours of dressing and makeup

Opening Night: The first performance of a new show or new cast for a live audience

Props: The accessories that performers use when acting, singing, and dancing that pertain to their roles and characters

Plot: The sequence of events in the drama that creates the meaning

Read-Throughs: A full cast rehearsal where every performer reads through his or her lines in the script with full expression and character

Rehearsal: The continuous, scheduled time period for practicing a script, show, or performance

Set: The materials and design that embody the stage and setting for a scene; the set often changes throughout the show

Setting: The place where the action in the story occurs

Tech Week: Typically the final week of rehearsals and the week preceding opening night, when the technical aspects of the show are rehearsed and finalized

Vignettes and Viewpoints

The following vignettes are modified excerpts of scenes from Broadway musicals, each focusing on a specific idea or event. These characters and settings are included, as they are strong examples of common themes in musicals: family and friendship, love and loss. When reading through the following examples, consider how you might use them in your own teaching. How are the characters feeling? What are the characters thinking? What story is being told?

As Lili entered the carnival grounds, she looked around her at the big, red and white striped tent, the decorated puppet booth, the magician's stand where his shiny black hat was resting on a table. She missed her father terribly and wished he was here with her, but she needed to show that she could move on, that she was growing up, even though she was only 16 years old. She had never traveled this far from her small, French village and did not know anyone here, except for the name on a piece of paper that her father had given her. A man who might give her a job. A man named Mr. Rodet. (From the musical Carnival!*)*

Galinda (Glinda the Good Witch) and Elphaba (the Wicked Witch of the West) have a difficult friendship. Galinda's striking appearance contrasts with Elphaba's green skin, they have opposing viewpoints on nearly every subject, and they have strong, but different, personalities. When they begin their studies at Shiz University, they discover that they have been assigned as roommates, an unfortunate but unchangeable situation. (From the musical Wicked*)*

After asking for an extra serving of food at the orphanage, Oliver is reprimanded and sold to a man who is an undertaker, forcing Oliver to sleep in the basement amongst coffins. This begins a troubled time for him, as he gets into fights with a bully and is almost locked in a coffin before being befriended by the Artful Dodger, who welcomes Oliver to join him where he lives and works (as a pickpocket). With the absence of any home or family, Oliver joins his new friend. (From the musical Oliver!*)*

Cosette is eight years old. She has been living in an inn with a family who expects her to clean and work all day long. She knows that these people are not her mother and father, and she dreams often of a woman who is nice to her, brings her peace, and loves her very much. Cosette remembers a time long ago when she did not have to work this hard, when she was warm and safe, in a place where she was taken care of and protected. (From the musical Les Misérables*)*

Musical Theater Activities for Energy and Entertainment

Musical theater elicits images of tap dancing, toe tapping, catchy songs, and beats. While some aspects of this art form invite self-reflection and the shared internal struggles of the characters in the show, musical theater is inherently a form of entertainment, meant to transport both performers and audience members to another place in time.

The activities in this section draw on three popular songs from three different musicals. Each imparts an important theme found through studies of musical theater participation—feelings, friendship, and performance—and is intended to energize your students, to build a sense of community, and to encourage interaction in large or small groups.

"Tomorrow" (from the musical *Annie*)

Pose the question to your students: If you could do anything, what you would do tomorrow? Ask students to share their ideas either in small or large group settings; they should include why this idea is important to them and how what they choose to do tomorrow may cause change over time. This activity can be done every week or once a month, focusing each time on a different theme or idea (such as helping the earth, personal goals, or a fantasy).

Skills—Students will learn to predict what may change tomorrow based on what choices they make today. This activity will give students a sense of empowerment, helping them to shape their own goals and also to recognize what needs to be accomplished first. Keep the activity open-ended. What will tomorrow bring? How do we know? How does that change what we want to do today? The ideas here are rooted in philosophy, but connecting this activity with the story of *Annie* and the song "Tomorrow" will help both younger and older students focus on what they can do in their lives now.

"Getting to Know You" (from the musical *The King and I*)

Pair students in the class, instructing each person to take a turn as the speaker. The first person to share will state three sentences about himself or herself, two of which have to be true, and one of which is false. The other student has to guess which sentence is untrue. Give students time to decide what it is they want to share about themselves, instructing them to present all three facts as truthfully as possible. The goal is to share new information but also to determine if the other person can identify what piece of information is untrue. This activity can be modified easily for younger students (focusing on identifying one aspect of the partner, such as a favorite color) and older grades (by increasing the number of sentences each student provides).

Skills—Students will learn to interact with all of the peers in their classroom, finding similarities and differences among them, taking the time to get to know their classmates. Although this works well at the beginning of the year, building this activity throughout the entire school year will assist students with forging friendships and developing a sense of classroom community.

> ### "Let Me Entertain You" (from the musical *Gypsy*)
>
> Provide students with a scene or scenario in which they have to improvise dialogue, music, or dance. It is helpful to create short scenes ahead of time from which students may select one to perform. This activity can be modified in many ways—students may participate as an entire class (half as performers, half as audience members), in small groups, or in pairs.
>
> Skills—This is perhaps a very difficult task (for children and adults alike), as improvising requires the ability to think on one's feet, be open to new ideas and suggestions, and focus on the scene to play off of the other performers' ideas. Encourage students to be supportive of one another, and participate if you can! Your involvement will encourage students to let go of their inhibitions.

Lessons and Assessments

The opening quote of this chapter, borrowed from the song "The Sound of Music" from the musical by the same name, is perhaps one of the most widely recognized lines from a musical theater production. The themes that prevail in this show include family and siblings, love and relationships, war and culture, and fear and hope. From one musical, many different concepts and perspectives can be explored, and the lessons presented in this section are built on those same themes.

Each lesson plan includes specific learning objectives pertaining to the related content areas and a focus on personal, social, and artistic learning. The assessments are diverse, including rubrics and checklists, worksheets and writing prompts, and several performance-based assessments (such as participating, contributing to activities, collaborating with peers, and engaging in the process of creating art).

Since musical theater does not have its own set of standards, the National Standards for Music, Theater, and Dance are referenced where relevant. The lessons following align with the standards for grades K–4 and the basic components of the standards for grades 5–8. Each lesson is also connected to the relevant core standards for early childhood education and elementary education and the Common Core standards for math and language arts.

This chapter has already referenced many musicals (from the most popular productions to lesser known shows), and the lessons here continue this trend. The lessons primarily draw upon a scene, a theme, or a song as the basis of the integrated lesson. The songs or excerpts that are drawn upon as the focal point of these lessons are readily available and easy to access through various online resources. I encourage you to read through all the lessons and to build your own repertoire of musical theater that may inspire you in ways this book only begins to explore. Even if it is not as grand as a Broadway production, your classroom will come alive with the sounds of musical theater.

Counting Cats

Content Areas: Musical Theater, Math

Grade Level: First

Learning Objectives

1. Students will estimate, compare, and sort the number of different cats in the musical.

2. Students will identify a relationship between the music and the interpretative behaviors and movements of the cats.

Standards

- National Standards for Music Education K–4
  - Content Standard 6—Achievement Standard(a)
- National Standards for Theater Education K–4
  - Content Standard 7—Achievement Standard(a)
- National Standards for Dance Education K–4
  - Content Standard 2—Achievement Standard(a)
- National Standards for Early Childhood Education
  - Standard 1(a)
  - Standard 3(c)
  - Standard 4(c)
- Common Core State Standards
  - 1.MD.4.

Procedures

This musical, by Andrew Lloyd Webber, was noted for being one of the longest running shows on Broadway. The focus of the show is on different cats, their names and purposes in their feline community, and the stories that each cat tells during the show. If possible, students should watch the entire production (or at least a significant video clip) to gather a full understanding of this show. Or rather than watching the entire musical, share a selected video clip or present an overview of the cast of characters in the show.

Have a discussion with students about what they observed—the different types of cats, costumes, and behaviors. Ask them if they can estimate how many cats were in the show and if they can think of a way to sort the cats. Have students discuss how the actors moved and acted like cats and what looked most accurate in their portrayal. How did the music relate to the actors' interpretation and make the characters feel like cats? Students could have the option of moving to the music on their own.

In small groups, have students explore the different cat families that are presented throughout the show (e.g., Jellicle cats, white cats, glamour cats), and compare these categories with actual cat families. Students should then create their own cats to be a part of the show, paying attention to accurate details about their felines' names, characteristics, and behaviors. Students should create a fictional cat and one that is grounded in realistic facts and features.

Extensions

The inspiration for this musical was a poem by T. S. Eliot entitled "The Naming of Cats" and a larger collection of poetry entitled *Old Possum's Book of Practical Cats*. Sharing this poem with your students is a nice way not only to extend this lesson but also to build upon the idea of how a musical is created.

Assessments

1. Students should actively engage in a discussion about the show and estimate the number of cats in the entire cast. Categorize students' predictions so that there is a class chart.

2. Individually, students should create their own cats for the show. One cat should fall into the fictional category of Jellicle cats and align with the theme of the musical, while the other should demonstrate students' knowledge of the characteristics and behaviors of actual cats and cat families.

How Many Trombones Are Too Many?

Content Areas: Musical Theater, Math, Language Arts

Grade Level: Fourth

Learning Objectives

1. Students will watch a clip of the song "76 Trombones" from the movie musical *The Music Man*.

2. Students will discuss imagery of having 76 trombones playing in one marching band.

3. Students will identify the relevance of 76 trombones in the song and interpret how Harold uses the idea of 76 trombones to trick the townspeople.

4. Students will create their own version of a marching band including specific numbers of instruments.

Standards

- National Standards for Music Education K–4
  - Content Standard 8—Achievement Standard(a)
  - Content Standard 9—Achievement Standard(a)
- National Standards for Elementary Education
  - Standard 2(2.3)(2.5)
  - Standard 3(3.1)(3.3)
- Common Core State Standards
  - 4.OA.5.

Procedures

Begin by sharing a short synopsis of the musical *The Music Man* with your students. The main character, Harold, is a con artist who visits a town posing as a band leader. He collects money to buy uniforms and instruments to start a band but quickly skips town with all the money. He uses the song "76 Trombones" to lure the townspeople into thinking he could have a really wonderful band. In reality, a marching band does not have more than a few trombones (sometimes a maximum of 10) at any one time.

Have students watch a clip of the song. (There are many online resources available for this, if needed.) Engage them in a discussion on the imagery of 76 trombones playing. Does it look real? What does it make you think of? How do you think the townspeople responded? Why would Harold have used 76 trombones instead of a different number or a different instrument? What is the relevance of the number 76?

Either individually or in small groups, students will create their own version of Harold's marching band, selecting an instrument that they want to focus on and determining the number of that instrument to be included in the envisioned band. Students should be able to support why they decided on a specific instrument (versus others) and how their change in the plot would impact the show's conclusion.

Extensions

This musical could be a platform for discussions on various subjects, such as the instruments in a marching band, instruments of the world, and the personality or characteristics of the protagonist in the show. The math connection here is intentionally a simple one, in that the goal is to have students think of numbers in different ways, such as how they are used here for a specific purpose.

Assessments

1. Much of the assessments can take place in small or large group discussions. Ensure that students are analyzing the show and the use of the number 76 for the number of trombones. Have each student document and present his or her own ideas and perspectives to you.

2. For the individual component, students should be encouraged to be creative! Have them explore and research different instruments and instrument families. Students should be able to describe what instrument would be their focus, why that instrument was selected, how many would be used in the band (and the relevance of their selected number), and how their idea might change the plot of the musical.

Many, Many Minutes

Content Areas: Musical Theater, Math

Grade Level: Fifth

Learning Objectives

1. Students will calculate the number of hours and days represented by 525,600 minutes.

2. Students will listen to the song "Seasons of Love" from the musical *Rent*.

3. Students will calculate another period of time and describe what they would accomplish during that time period.

Standards

- National Standards for Music Education 5–8
  - o Content Standard 6—Achievement Standard(a)
  - o Content Standard 9—Achievement Standard(a)
- National Standards for Elementary Education
  - o Standard 2(2.3)(2.5)
  - o Standard 3(3.4)
  - o Standard 4(4.0)
- Common Core State Standards
  - o 5.MD.1.

Procedures

The musical *Rent* was popular for its realistic themes of drug abuse, gender identity, and disease. The focus of this lesson, however, is on one song in the musical that talks of the dreams of all the characters by asking the question: What can be accomplished in 525,600 minutes, and how do we measure love?

It is important here to have students listen to the song after they have calculated and identified the various time periods equivalent to 525,600 minutes—because the song gives away the answer! The song should then be the starting point for a discussion on the relevance of this number of minutes and on using units of time in a new way. Try also to focus on the ideas and concepts described in the lyrics.

Students will then individually consider another time period and what might be accomplished during that time. The idea is to follow the theme of calculating minutes (or any smaller units of time), so the number representing the new time period should be large, and the period itself should not be easily identifiable from the number.

Extensions

Having students share their ideas would make a wonderful class discussion on the ways in which we can manipulate numbers to be something they do not necessarily seem and why someone would choose to do so. The concept of manipulating units of time can also be transferred to any other lesson or subject area.

Assessments

Students' final ideas and calculations are the main assessment for this lesson. Have students give a short presentation/description of their idea (to compare/contrast with their classmates) and also submit a more detailed written description. Encourage students to think broadly and differently about numbers—to look at numbers and units of time in new ways.

Over the Rainbow

Content Areas: Musical Theater, Science

Grade Level: Kindergarten

Learning Objectives

1. Students will listen to and watch the song "Somewhere Over the Rainbow" from the movie musical *The Wizard of Oz.*

2. Students will identify some characteristics of rainbows and discuss why Dorothy dreams of going "over the rainbow."

3. Students will describe what they might like to do if they could travel to a distant place.

Standards

- National Standards for Music Education K–4
  - o Content Standard 6—Achievement Standard(b)
  - o Content Standard 8—Achievement Standard(a)
- National Standards for Early Childhood Education
  - o Standard 1(b)(c)
  - o Standard 4(c)

Procedures

Begin the discussion by asking students if they have ever seen a rainbow. What did it look like? Was it far away? What might be beyond the rainbow? Play the song (preferably a video clip), and ask students to discuss what Dorothy was describing. Can there really be something beyond a rainbow? Categorize the students' responses.

Ask students to also describe the characteristics of a rainbow (such as shape, colors, and relevant weather conditions). Explain that Dorothy was dreaming about traveling to a different place, somewhere far from home. Ask students to imagine where they might travel if they had the chance. Why would they pick that place? How would they get there?

Extensions

To build on the musical elements of this lesson, students could even provide suggestions (one or two sentences from their own ideas) that would together compose a class song. This would be a new version of the song "Somewhere Over the Rainbow" with the students' ideas.

Assessments

While a class discussion is an informal way to observe student understanding, students could also complete the Over the Rainbow Worksheet. Here students should color in the rainbow with appropriate colors and draw an image of what they would do if they traveled over the rainbow. The teacher can also write a brief sentence of the students' description.

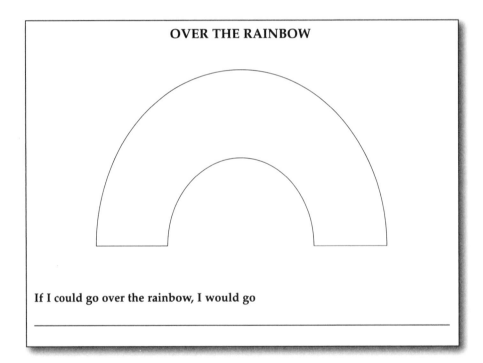

OVER THE RAINBOW

If I could go over the rainbow, I would go

Singin' and Dancin' in the Rain

Content Areas: Musical Theater, Science

Grade Level: Third

Learning Objectives

1. Students will watch the song "Singin' in the Rain" from the movie musical of the same name.

2. Students will identify how the elements of weather create the atmosphere for the song and for the actors.

3. Students will create their own version of the song and describe what kind of weather will be the focus, why it is important, and how it would impact their staging of the song.

Standards

- National Standards for Music Education K–4
  - Content Standard 4—Achievement Standard(b)
  - Content Standard 6—Achievement Standard(c)
- National Standards for Theater Education K–4
  - Content Standard 3—Achievement Standard(a)
- National Standards for Dance Education K–4
  - Content Standard 3—Achievement Standard(a)
  - Content Standard 4—Achievement Standard(a)
- National Standards for Early Childhood Education
  - Standard 1(a)
  - Standard 3(a)
  - Standard 4(c)

Procedures

Play the video clip of the song "Singin' in the Rain" (from the movie musical) and ask students to describe their perceptions of the song. What did they observe? How were the actors singing and dancing? What impact did the rain have on the song and performance? Ask students to consider how important the rain is for the song—it is mentioned in the title, but what if there were some other weather that was the focus?

In small groups or individually, have students brainstorm ideas for other weather conditions that could be the focus of the song. Students should also consider what changes would be made in the choreography and staging of the song. Additionally, they should consider how a different type of weather would impact the actors' performances.

Extensions

If time permits, having students collaborate to perform their ideas would be a wonderful extension of this activity! This lesson is truly a combination of music, theater, and dance integrated with science, so extend this activity based on upon your available time to build this lesson.

Assessments

Students should respond to the following prompts. Students should elaborate with details supporting their ideas, particularly when describing how the change in weather will impact the entire song.

The song will be changed to "_____ in the Rain," because _____

This weather will change the way the actors dance because _____

This weather will make the actors feel _____

The mood of the song will become _____

The setting for the song will be changed to _____

Elements of Ecosystems

Content Areas: Musical Theater, Science

Grade Level: Fourth

Learning Objectives

1. Students will watch excerpts of the movie musical *The Lion King*.

2. Students will identify the various ecosystems presented throughout the musical.

3. Students will describe the importance of the ecosystems for the animals featured in the musical. Students should also discuss the components of the physical environment and the human impact on the ecosystems.

Standards

- National Standards for Theater Education K–4
  - Content Standard 2—Achievement Standard(a)
  - Content Standard 3—Achievement Standard(a)
- National Standards for Elementary Education
  - Standard 2(2.2)(2.5)
  - Standard 3(3.1)(3.3)

Procedures

Based on the allotted time for this lesson, students should watch either selected video clips or the entire movie musical *The Lion King*. Students should document the various ecosystems that appear in the film, noting the animals that are highlighted in each setting.

Have a discussion with students over what they observed. What were the primary ecosystems featured in the movie? Which animals thrived in certain settings? What was the importance of the different ecosystems to the animals and to the different settings in the musical?

In small groups or individually, students should chart/document the various ecosystems presented in the film. Students should also categorize the animals that appeared and their placement on the food chain. Many animals make recurring appearances and move between different ecosystems in the film. Students should also consider their own role in impacting ecosystems.

Extensions

Since *The Lion King* was first a hugely successful animated movie, the lesson could be built from video clips. However, the smash Broadway musical presents an entirely different experience—a new perspective on and interpretation of the movie. If possible, students should watch the musical to understand how the presence of actors and a live stage impacts the physical environment of the performance.

Assessments

There are many ways that this lesson could be assessed. Ideally, students should complete an individual chart or document that shows their understanding of the different ecosystems and the relationships between the animals that live there. Encourage students to be creative in their presentations while still ensuring they include all the necessary components.

What a Beautiful Mornin'!

Content Areas: Musical Theater, Science, Social Studies

Grade Level: Fifth Grade

Learning Objectives

1. Students will listen to the song "Oh! What a Beautiful Mornin'" from the musical *Oklahoma!*

2. Students will identify the various fields and the crops that were grown in America in the early 1900s.

3. Students will describe the resurgence of farming and the development of agriculture in America from the year 1906.

Standards

- National Standards for Music Education 5–8
  - o Content Standard 6—Achievement Standard(a)
  - o Content Standard 9—Achievement Standard(a)
- National Standards for Theater Education 5–8
  - o Content Standard 5—Achievement Standard(a)
- National Standards for Elementary Education
  - o Standard 2(2.2)(2.5)
  - o Standard 3(3.1)(3.3)

Procedures

Begin the lesson by either playing the song or showing students a video clip of the song. Ask students to describe their impressions of the song, the lyrics, and the setting. Many of the video clips have the song staged in a large, open cornfield. How does this relate to the song and the times?

Continue the discussion by addressing the setting of the musical—Oklahoma during the early 1900s. Ask students to research the crops that were a focus of the times, why they were important to the farming industry, and how they impacted the environment.

The focus of students' discussion and research should be on how the farming industry led to the development of agriculture in America during this time. Another question to consider is whether the representations of this time period are accurate in the musical.

A wonderful resource is the Oklahoma Historical Society's *Encyclopedia of Oklahoma History and Culture*, which can be found through the following link: http://digital.library.okstate.edu/encyclo pedia/entries/F/FA019.html.

Extensions

Studying and understanding agriculture is an important component of the fifth grade curriculum, and this song and musical are great starting points for this discussion. However, this lesson could also be modified by talking about any region—use the song to introduce the topic, and build upon it by discussing agriculture around the world.

Assessments

Students should prepare a presentation—written, verbal, or in some other form—that allows them to share their research and findings. Students should build connections between the setting in the musical and the relevance of farming and crops during the early 1900s in America.

The Von Trapp Family

Content Areas: Musical Theater, Social Studies, Math

Grade Level: First

Learning Objectives

1. Students will watch a short clip from the movie musical *The Sound of Music* and identify the family dynamics of the Von Trapp family.

2. Students will list the members of their own families.

3. Students will compare and contrast their own families with the Von Trapp family and the families of their classmates.

Standards

- National Standards for Music Education K–4
  o Content Standard 9—Achievement Standard(b)
- National Standards for Theater Education K–4
  o Content Standard 7—Achievement Standard(a)
- National Standards for Early Childhood Education
  o Standard 1(a)
  o Standard 4(b)(c)

Procedures

After watching a video clip from the musical *The Sound of Music*, engage students in a discussion on the dynamics of the Von Trapp Family. Ask students to describe what they observed about the Von Trapp family—the number of individuals, their genders, and their ages. Have students describe their own families, noting immediate similarities and differences.

In small groups, have students work together to share information about their families and then compare and contrast them. (This can be done with teacher supervision.) In a large group, chart students' family members, asking students to compare and contrast through their own observations.

Extensions

As a side note, four siblings who are descendants of Captain Von Trapp have collaborated to create a singing group aptly named the Von Trapp Children. It would be interesting for your students to know that the story of *The Sound of Music* was based upon a real family!

Assessments

Students should document their own family members and document/chart the family members of at least two classmates. The ways in which students present this information can vary; they can use individual, artistic documentation, or use small group collaboration.

What's Important in Friendship?

Content Areas: Musical Theater, Social Studies

Grade Level: Second

Learning Objectives

1. Students will watch/listen to the song "Friendship" from the musical *Anything Goes.*

2. Students will identify the various characteristics of friendship as presented in the song's lyrics and choreography.

3. Students will describe what qualities they believe make a good friend and are important in friendship.

Standards

- National Standards for Music Education K–4
  - Content Standard 6—Achievement Standard(b)
- National Standards for Dance Education K–4
  - Content Standard 3—Achievement Standard(a)
- National Standards for Early Childhood Education
  - Standard 1(a)
  - Standard 3(b)
  - Standard 4(b)(c)

Procedures

The song "Friendship" from the musical *Anything Goes* is a pivotal number in the musical and one that has been performed in many different settings. After students watch a video clip or listen to the song, ask them to discuss what qualities of friendship are described in the song.

Build on this discussion by having students contribute their own ideas for friendship. What do they believe is important in friendship? What makes a good friend? How do we build friendships with new people? Have students work in small groups and share their ideas for friendship, comparing and contrasting their views with those of their classmates. Additional questions should explore how the song describes friendship and how dance is a social activity.

Extensions

Having students rewrite the lyrics to the song (perhaps in a small group or pairs) would give them greater ownership over this lesson. Adding an informal performance component would also take this activity to another level!

Assessments

Students should present their ideas for what defines friendship in a creative format. Some suggestions include writing a song or poem or making a visual presentation or display. Their ideas could be presented in pairs or small groups, if students collaborate to define what friendship means.

Getting to Know You!

Content Areas: Musical Theater, Social Studies

Grade Level: Third

Learning Objectives

1. Students will watch/listen to the song "Getting to Know You" from the musical *The King and I*.

2. Students will identify the characteristics of the Thai culture as presented in the movie (where Thailand is often referred to as Siam) and compare that with a more accurate representation of Thailand in contemporary times.

3. Students will discuss the challenges of meeting new people and building friendships with people in another country.

Standards

- National Standards for Music Education K–4
  - o Content Standard 6—Achievement Standards(a)(b)(c)
- National Standards for Theater Education K–4
  - o Content Standard 7—Achievement Standard(a)
- National Standards for Early Childhood Education
  - o Standard 2(a)
  - o Standard 3(b)
  - o Standard 4(a)(b)

Procedures

Have students listen to or watch a video clip of the song "Getting to Know You" from the musical *The King and I*. Ask students to discuss what they are observing, the interactions between actors, and the descriptions in the lyrics of the song.

Build on this discussion by asking students to describe the Thai culture and the characteristics of the environment, setting, and costumes presented in the musical. Note that many of the depictions are dated—the play opened on Broadway in 1951, and the film was made in 1956—so this is just a good starting point for discussing different cultures. Provide students with more current representations of modern Thai culture so that they are aware of the differences between the present day and the time when the musical was produced.

Engage students in a discussion about differences between their cultures and the Thai culture (or build on comparing other different cultures). What are some of the similarities and differences? How might it be difficult to make friends with someone in a different culture, and why?

Extensions

If possible, students could use the Internet to find pen pals from a different country. The focus in this activity should not be just about making friends; it should be on comparing different cultures and recognizing the challenges of meeting new people.

Assessments

Have students draft a letter to someone from a different country (of their choosing). The letter should include all the components that are listed in the objectives of this lesson, such as recognizing the different characteristics of the two cultures and the challenges of meeting new people, as well as what they would need to do in order to get to know this new person.

Generations X, Y, and Z

Content Areas: Musical Theater, Social Studies

Grade Level: Fifth

Learning Objectives

1. Students will listen to the song "Chop Suey" from the musical *Flower Drum Song*.

2. Students will define the concept of generations as presented in the song and interpret the song's meanings.

3. Students will compare and contrast their perspectives on two different generations with those of a family member.

Standards

- National Standards for Music Education 5–8
  - Content Standard 6—Achievement Standard(a)
  - Content Standard 9—Achievement Standard(a)
- National Standards for Elementary Education
  - Standard 2(2.4)(2.5)
  - Standard 3(3.1)(3.3)

Procedures

Play the song "Chop Suey" for your students, and ask them to reflect on what the lyrics say and the meaning of the song. Have students share their ideas with the class, and discuss the theme of generations that is a focus of the song. Ask students what generations they have in their families and how they would define a generation.

Students will then discuss the theme of generation with an older family member. Students will focus on how they define a generation and on how they view this family member's generation (such as the food, songs, and activities that are popular with members of this different generation). Students will also document the older family members' perspectives so there are two contrasting views. This information should then be shared with the class, either as a whole or in small groups.

Note: Some versions of this song mention a Maidenform bra as part of the lyrics, and it is up to you if you choose to edit those lyrics or play only a portion of the song as a platform for discussions on generations.

Extensions

A larger extension of this lesson would be to look at generations from a cross-cultural perspective. The focus of the song is on one generation's view of another, but it looks also at themes related to different lifestyles and homelands.

Assessments

Students should define the concept of a generation and what it means to be a part of a generation. How is their generation viewed by others? What items, places, music, and food do they feel define their own generation? These questions should be explored in their descriptions, which should include both their individual perspectives on their generation and those of an older family member.

What Is Happiness?

Content Areas: Musical Theater, Language Arts

Grade Level: Kindergarten

Learning Objectives

1. Students will listen to the song "Happiness" from the musical *You're a Good Man Charlie Brown*.

2. Students will identify the characteristics of begin happy as described in the lyrics of the song.

3. Students will share their own ideas for what makes them happy and compare their ideas with those of their classmates.

Standards

- National Standards for Music Education K–4
  - Content Standard 6—Achievement Standards(b)(c)
- National Standards for Early Childhood Education
  - Standard 1(a)
  - Standard 3(a)(b)
- Common Core State Standards
  - SL.K.6.

Procedures

Briefly ask students what it means to be happy and what makes them happy. Then play an audio or video clip of the song "Happiness" from the musical *You're a Good Man Charlie Brown*. Continue the discussion with students by asking them how the characters in the song described happiness. Document all the students' responses.

Individually, students should then think of what makes them happy—either a person, a place, or an activity. Each student should describe her or his own idea of happiness to the class.

Extensions

This activity (and song) is a great springboard for a discussion on feelings. Build on the topic of happiness, and ask students to consider what makes them sad, angry, excited, and scared. Encourage discussions about these feelings at home and in the classroom to build social awareness and students' abilities to consider alternative perspectives.

Assessments

Students can share their responses with the class or individually with the teacher. A nice supplement would be to complete the Happiness Worksheet.

Happiness Is . . .

Up and Down the Beanstalk

Content Areas: Musical Theater, Language Arts

Grade Level: First

Learning Objectives

1. Students will listen to the song "Giants in the Sky" from the musical *Into the Woods*.

2. Students will discuss Jack's perspective in the story of having climbed the beanstalk.

3. Students will interpret the song and discuss their own perceptions of the lyrics.

Standards

- National Standards for Music Education K–4
  - Content Standard 6—Achievement Standard(c)
- National Standards for Early Childhood Education
  - Standard 3(a)(b)
  - Standard 4(b)(c)
- Common Core State Standards
  - RL.1.1.
  - RL.1.3.
  - SL.1.1.

Procedures

After they have listened to the song "Giants in the Sky," ask students to discuss who is the narrator in the song and what story is being told. Document students' ideas and contributions, particularly those that are focused on the story of Jack and the Beanstalk. Explain that this song is from the musical entitled *Into the Woods*, which is about many different fairy tale characters' adventures. (You could choose to play a larger video clip of the musical so that students will understand the context of the song.)

Ask students to discuss what they believe the song means. What is Jack saying? What did he experience up the beanstalk? Who are the giants he is referring to, and are there really giants in the sky? Build on this discussion by having students consider Jack's perspective. What was it like climbing a beanstalk? What were the challenges? Was he scared or brave?

Extensions

This lesson could be a starting point for a lesson or greater discussion on fact versus fiction. Use the famous literary characters in fairy tales as examples, and ask students to consider these characters' alternative perspectives.

Assessments

The goal of this activity is to have students consider alternative perspectives. Students should discuss/share/write their ideas about how Jack must have felt while going up the beanstalk, and contrast that perspective with their own. This could be done through large or small group discussions, informal presentations or performances, or the creation of a short poem that highlights this duality.

Dr. Seuss's Musical

Content Areas: Musical Theater, Language Arts

Grade Level: Second

Learning Objectives

1. Students will listen to or watch an excerpt of the musical *Seussical*.

2. Students will discuss the various stories and characters presented in the excerpt (or focus on one book's theme).

3. Students will present their own poems inspired by one of the Dr. Seuss books presented in the musical.

Standards

- National Standards for Music Education K–4
  - o Content Standard 6—Achievement Standard(b)
- National Standards for Theater Education K–4
  - o Content Standard 7—Achievement Standard(b)
- National Standards for Early Childhood Education
  - o Standard 3(a)
  - o Standard 4(b)(c)
- Common Core State Standards
  - o RL.2.4.
  - o RI.2.4.
  - o SL.2.5.

Procedures

Based on the works of Dr. Seuss, *Seussical the Musical* is a narrative told by the Cat in the Hat about the various different characters highlighted in Dr. Seuss's books. Choose a clip or song that you feel is relevant for your students to watch. (Your choice is limited only by the amount of time you have for this activity; the whole show is completely appropriate for younger audiences.) Students should discuss what they observe, including the staging, characters, and stories that are presented.

Ask students questions about how the characters are related to one another in the musical. After a class discussion, students should gather in small groups to further discuss and brainstorm their ideas. Some questions they should consider include the following: What are common themes in the stories that are highlighted in the musical? What is the role of poetry in Dr. Seuss's books and in the songs?

Each student should then individually create a poem that is influenced by Dr. Seuss's works. This could be a poem that is written in the same style as his writings, or one that includes or highlights a specific Dr. Seuss character.

Extensions

This lesson could be a platform for further discussions on poetry, types of poetry, and how Dr. Seuss used poetry and rhyming in his books.

There are some wonderful resources for submitting and publishing students' poetry online. Many of these services provide online publication for free and also offer paper publications of student work for purchase.

Assessments

In addition to actively participating in large and small group discussions, students' poems could be collected and documented in a class book or displayed in a related presentation. Dr. Seuss's writing and rhyming style was unique and noted for its simplicity. Encourage students to use this style when creating their own poems.

Defining a Definition

Content Areas: Musical Theater, Language Arts

Grade Level: Third

Learning Objectives

1. Students will listen to or watch an excerpt from the musical *The 25th Annual Putnam County Spelling Bee.*

2. Students will create their own word and a definition for it.

Standards

- National Standards for Music Education K–4
  - Content Standard 6—Achievement Standard(b)
- National Standards for Early Childhood Education
  - Standard 1(a)
  - Standard 4(b)(c)
- Common Core State Standards
  - RF.3.3.

Procedures

The 25th Annual Putnam County Spelling Bee is a musical that highlights the excitement and anxiety students experience when participating in a national spelling bee. Some of the songs are more appropriate for older audiences, while many are suited for early elementary students. The opening number is a great example of the latter; in it, audience members are actually invited to participate in the production.

Ask students to reflect on the challenges of a spelling bee (or if they have ever participated in one). How do you prepare for a spelling bee? What is more important—taking part in the experience, or winning the competition? Students should then discuss some of their own vocabulary words (as included in the existing curriculum) and brainstorm ideas for creating their own words and definitions.

Extensions

If the class has not had a spelling bee before, this lesson would be a wonderful starting point for arranging a small-scaled, classroom spelling bee.

Assessments

Each student should create his or her own word and definition. The word should have actual meaning related to its root word (as used in spelling bees); for example, it could have a Latin or Greek root. Students should be able to define the word within a context and use it appropriately in a sentence. This could be part of a larger creative writing activity or something novel for students to share with their peers. Encourage students to reference the dictionary for common prefix and root words; it is a great resource for this lesson.

Analyzing Annie

Content Areas: Musical Theater, Language Arts

Grade Level: Fourth

Learning Objectives

1. Students will listen to or watch the songs "Hard Knock Life" and/or "Tomorrow" from the musical *Annie*.

2. Students will collaborate to interpret the meanings of the songs.

3. Students will discuss the songs by considering their own perspectives and perceptions.

Standards

- National Standards for Music Education K–4
  - o Content Standard 6—Achievement Standards(a)(b)
  - o Content Standard 8—Achievement Standard(a)
  - o Content Standard 9—Achievement Standard(c)
- National Standards for Elementary Education
  - o Standard 2(2.1)(2.5)
  - o Standard 3(3.3)(3.4)(3.5)
- Common Core State Standards
  - o RL.4.2.
  - o RL.4.3.
  - o RL.4.6.

Procedures

The musical *Annie* is perhaps one of the most famous musicals about children. Many of your students will be familiar with this musical, while others will find it a new topic. Select between the two songs "Hard Knock Life" and "Tomorrow," or use both in two parallel activities. Play the song(s) for your students, and ask them to discuss the meanings of the lyrics. What is the story being told? What is Annie describing in the song?

Document students' ideas, and build on this initial discussion. Distribute copies of the lyrics, and ask students to consider Annie's perspective. Why would she sing about this topic (what does "hard knock" mean, or what is she hoping for the next day?) Students should analyze the themes in the song, consider the different points of view presented, and discuss how they use music in their lives.

Extensions

To build on the musical elements of this lesson, students could write their own lyrics to the song "Tomorrow" (either individually or as a class) and perform it with the new lyrics. Collaborative performances such as these provide students with a sense of ownership over their work and opportunities to work with their peers in a creative context.

Assessments

Students should each individually write a narrative or create some alternative presentation about what Annie's life was like. Themes that should be considered are the struggles she endured while working, how she experienced loneliness, and her aspirations for friends and a family. Students' submissions should also include their own perceptions of Annie's feelings and a consideration of their own lives and settings in relation to Annie's.

PART III

Behind the Curtain

7

Building Artistic Connections

Integrating the performing arts requires enthusiasm, motivation, time, commitment, planning, and scheduling, but implementation is both challenging and rewarding. Although it may seem that you are the only one invested in this project when you begin, it is noteworthy to recognize how you can find and utilize support systems for the performing arts within the school, home, and community settings.

This chapter discusses various resources and references for building artistic connections within the school, among families, and within the community settings. The idea here is that while the process of integrating the performing arts may begin within one classroom, these experiences can be augmented by fostering relationships with other individuals. This includes grade-level teachers, administrators, arts specialists, family members and siblings who are invested in these projects, and arts organizations and performance venues in neighboring communities.

You may be fortunate to have an abundance of resources and materials, an administration that supports the performing arts, and a school rich with artistic experiences for students. Alternatively, you may find that your experiences resonate with those of the thousands of teachers whose settings are a stark contrast to such an ideal—a place where funding is scarce, resources are depleted, and a stronger focus is placed on successful test taking than on engaging in the creative process.

The ideas presented throughout this chapter are broad in scope, recognizing that every school and community setting is unique. Building artistic connections is a long-term process, one that can transform integrated performing arts activities from individual events into collaborative experiences.

School Connections

Elliott Eisner brilliantly noted that "The arts' position in the school curriculum symbolizes to the young what adults believe is important" (Eisner, 1999). When music, theater, dance, and musical theater permeate the entire school, students are more likely to believe that these activities are a valued and meaningful part of their educational experiences.

In my years of visiting, observing, and speaking with teachers about integrating the performing arts, I have consistently found that the school climate can profoundly impact any integrated arts activities. In some settings, the entire school engages in arts integration, adding these experiences as a necessary and vital part of the curriculum. Contrastingly, a teacher who wants to bring the performing arts into the classroom finds even greater challenges when the administration is unsupportive or other teachers do not find value in these experiences.

Connecting With Teachers

The best place to begin is often with the other teachers in the school. Whether or not teachers are currently integrating the arts into their own classrooms, it is worthwhile to have conversations during grade-level meetings to discuss ideas for creating and implementing lessons that would involve more than one classroom. Teachers' familiarity with their own curriculum and the activities taking place in, for example, the "other first-grade classroom" marks a logical first step in bridging connections outside of one classroom setting.

Grade-level discussions also allow for a shared platform for designing lessons. Teachers in the same grade levels are best aware of the challenges their colleagues face, the strengths of their position, and the topics that are mandated for the curriculum. One idea is to take a series of relevant performing arts lessons and implement them one class at a time. Another suggestion is to use the lessons as a starting point for creating a gradewide unit centered on an appropriate theme and designed by all the teachers as a collaborative project.

Similarly, many teachers have shared with me how the richest discussions come from conversations with teachers in other grade levels. While the specific learning objectives or assessments are not necessarily applicable, the talking points and ideas serve as a foundation for building one's own repertoire of songs, scripts, and dances; finding new ways to collaborate (perhaps by engaging older students as mentors to younger ones); and integrating the performing arts.

Connecting With Arts Specialists

Observation hours are required for an arts methods course that I teach every quarter, and a student once shared with me her excitement at observing a music teacher in a preschool. In a majority of preschool and kindergarten classrooms, the classroom teacher is responsible for integrating the arts (and this is often expected as part of this grade-level curriculum). My student was thrilled at the prospect that the preschoolers in this unique school setting were provided with a 30-minute music class once a week *with a music teacher*—it wasn't much, she said, but it was clear the children loved it and looked forward to it.

It is no secret that when a school has financial constraints (as many do today), arts programs are the first to be eliminated, perhaps because they are perceived as lacking value or as not being a necessary component of education. When this unfortunate and common occurrence takes place, the arts specialists—music, theater, dance, and visual arts teachers—are, too, removed from the schools.

In my conversations with arts specialists who are teaching in major cities around the United States, many have described their frustrations and feelings of alienation from the schools they work in, being perceived as valuable only because they provide free time for other teachers (when the arts specialists are working with those teachers' students), and feeling that their work with children in the arts is not considered valuable. Drawing upon these viewpoints, it becomes evident that it is important to consider how teachers who are beginning to integrate the performing arts into their own classrooms feel the same way—isolated and overwhelmed with the task at hand. Connecting with the music, theater, or dance teacher in a school is a wonderful way to build a natural collaboration, to draw upon the arts specialist's expertise and resources to bring the performing arts into your own classroom.

Connecting With Schools

The best place to begin building any artistic connection is within your own school setting, to move beyond one classroom, to utilize the resources around you, and to collaborate with the teachers and arts specialists who can help establish a learning environment that is rich with integrated performing arts experiences.

Do you have an afterschool program for students who want to participate in the arts, or for children who are at a high risk for academic failure? What are the characteristics of your program that are successful? What are the weaknesses? Perhaps most important, are there neighboring schools with which you can collaborate to build these programs and provide more resources and venues for the students involved? Most often, afterschool programs with wonderful goals and visions struggle because they are led by one teacher with limited resources and supplies. Going out into the community to find similar programs is a great way to start to augment an existing program and build connections with other teachers and students. An added benefit is shared resources and materials.

A unique, collaborative initiative by the John F. Kennedy Center for the Performing Arts in Washington, DC, brought musical theater into two middle schools. Through this program, teachers, teaching artists, and students collaborated to present productions of *Aladdin, Jr.* and *Mulan, Jr.* with the students as the performers in both shows. Importantly, both middle schools performed both productions, with each school taking turns using the same sets, staging, props, accessories, scripts, and music.

How might a similar collaboration take place in your own setting? What elementary, middle, or secondary schools are located nearby? One aspect to consider is that a benefit of connecting with elementary charter or private schools is that these settings often have designated funding for arts programs for students. Tapping into these resources is a way to find support for your own activities. Similarly, middle and secondary schools also have arts programs (both during and after school) for students, and connecting with teachers in these settings can provide you with access to a variety of costumes, props, scenery, music, and scripts. In some instances, older students may also assume leadership roles by assisting with your elementary students' productions.

Neighboring universities and colleges with music, theater, dance, or performing arts programs are also valuable resources for your own activities. Professors are often eager to connect with schools, to build programs, and explore partnership opportunities. In addition to borrowing materials, consider requesting minimal use of space for performances (either informal or formal), as institutions of higher education often have wonderful venues for sharing artistic experiences.

Home Connections

It was two weeks before our big spring musical revue, and the costumes that had been specially ordered for this performance were backordered and delayed. I was informed that the intricately designed outfits would be shipped and delivered a week after our performance. I was panicking, and the students were upset. I sent out a letter to parents asking if they knew of any resources or contacts, and I called neighboring schools and organizations for supplies.

The following morning, I received a call from a mother of one of my students, who stated she read my letter and would be more than happy to assist our class with costumes. She was, in fact, the lead costume designer for a local children's theater, and while some of the costumes needed to be made, several could be borrowed from the theater's existing wardrobe. The costumes she obtained for us were glorious, and I was able to negotiate a refund for the ones that shipped late. I could not have asked for a better ending to this story.

Connecting With Families

Families are a vital resource for any school and program. Just as I learned, you never know if a parent, family member, relative, or sibling has access to valuable resources. In the situation described in the above vignette, not only did I build a connection with the parent (who received full recognition for her work), but I also made connections with the children's theater, from which my students often borrowed costumes and where they watched live performances.

As a music teacher, I often contend that my students are my greatest source of building a repertoire. Borrowing the music and songs that students listen to at home is a simple way to build a home–school connection. Invite parents into the classroom to observe and experience performing arts activities with you and your students. Stories abound in the news of schools that shut down arts programs and parents who joined with teachers to protest these eliminations and save the arts for the students. Firsthand participation is much more effective than just sharing stories through e-mails and newsletters. Involving families will garner much needed support for your activities and programs.

Parents, siblings, and relatives may also work or be affiliated with organizations and companies that can sponsor, donate to, or support your programs. Funding from these sources is more easily obtained than grants or donations from government organizations. The added benefit is the personal connection forged with your students' families.

Connecting as Volunteers

Integrating the performing arts includes many different components, from planning to the actual implementation of a project—particularly for projects that are large in scale and performance. It is logical to gather volunteers and support from students' families and from staff and administration throughout the school. In fact, many community theaters actually require parental involvement for a child to be cast in a show. Utilize family members to help implement any activity, lesson, or larger production. Create and distribute a list of activities to encourage parents to sign up for committees throughout the year. Such a list might include service on committees for music, makeup, costumes, choreography, tickets, seating, refreshments, instruments, lighting, and sound. Create a list of what *you* need most.

You will be surprised at how involved family members will want to be with the performing arts activities you introduce. These settings are often an outlet for the untapped performer to be a part of a show, to bring in instruments, or to dance with the class. In one amazing example, the father of one of my students invited my students to record a compilation of songs as a class project in his small, in-home recording studio. This wonderful opportunity may never have presented itself if I did not take the initiative to ask parents about their interests in becoming involved in our performing arts activities.

Community Connections

One of the oldest beliefs in educational philosophy is that the community plays a large role in shaping, influencing, and ultimately supporting the schools. Organizations and artists, educational researchers and scholars, are all charged with supporting schools, collaborating with teachers, and engaging students in unique, hands-on experiences. With that in mind, how can you turn to the organizations and individuals within your own community for resources that will shape music, theater, dance, and musical theater in your classroom?

Connecting With Arts Organizations

A large number of performing arts centers and arts organizations have dedicated educational outreach programs focused on connecting with students, teachers, and schools. In fact, many sustained integrated arts programs and projects are the results of successful partnerships between schools and arts organizations. If your school or setting does not currently have such a partnership in place, consider contacting a local organization whose goals are focused on an area of performing arts that you are interested in. For example, The Lyric Opera of Chicago has opera programs for elementary students, and Carnegie Hall in New York has a music curriculum for second and third graders. In addition to developing a full-scale partnership, you may be able to implement portions of a lesson or activity with the support of the arts organization, or utilize its educational materials or performance venues for your class.

Connecting With Guest Artists

One of the greatest experiences for elementary students is when a guest speaker visits the class to share firsthand accounts of a particular trade, job, or endeavor. Similarly, the guest artists and teaching artists who visit and collaborate with classroom teachers (some freelance and others through arts organizations) provide students with a unique perspective on the arts, hands-on participation, and an opportunity to take ownership over their work. Examples of these include a dance specialist teaching free movement with a class of fifth graders in a high-risk, urban school; a theater teacher engaging English language learners in a fourth-grade class of students whose primary languages include Mandarin and Hindi; and a music teacher bringing a variety of stringed instruments (ranging from a banjo to a sitar) for a class of kindergarteners to explore.

Conversations with the students, teachers, and teaching artists in these examples mirrored one another. There was a consistent desire to extend and continue these experiences. Among students, there was a notable increase in motivation to attend school and participate in activities. Among classroom teachers, there was consistent enthusiasm for these unique collaborations.

While some artists may visit these classes as volunteers, it is important to recognize that such visits are an additional source of funding for their own artistic endeavors, and so many may require stipends for their visits. Allocating a small amount of funds each year for these types of artistic connections may allow for only one or two visits, but these visits will surely make a lasting impression on your students.

Connecting at Live Performances

Most every performing artist will assert the value of experiencing a live performance of a practiced group of performers in a public venue. While the performing arts have a valued and meaningful place in the classroom, the opportunity to see a live show or sit in the audience of a grand performance hall is one that many students may never experience. Many educators have written about the audience experience, the learning that takes place when watching a live show (see Reason, 2010), and the importance of these perspectives for students' understanding and appreciation of the performing arts.

Scheduling and planning a field trip seems the ideal choice for implementing this type of opportunity, but many schools do not have funding for such trips, nor are all parents able to provide financial support or additional expenses for school activities. Importantly, the same arts organizations and performance venues that have educational outreach programs often provide discounted or free performances for schools. In fact, many venues allow audience members to watch dress rehearsals free of charge. At these performances, students may also have the chance to meet the performers, explore the stage and set, or observe the interactions backstage, giving an entirely new dimension to their understanding of the performing arts.

Maintaining Connections

The ideas presented in this chapter are meant as starting points for supporting your integrated performing arts programs. The examples of organizations, artists, and venues will clearly vary in each community, but the goal here is to try to build and maintain a partnership that will inform artistic opportunities for your students.

As you shape the role of the performing arts in your classroom, create two lists—one of immediate needs, and one of idealistic hopes. Share these with the individuals you speak with, the artists who visit your classroom, and the organizations who open their doors to your students. While these connections are not requisite for integrating the performing arts, collaborative opportunities will provide multiple resources for you and your students and continue to foster the shared experiences inherent to the performing arts.

8

The Artistically Reflective Teacher

To know how to suggest is the great art of teaching

—Ralph Waldo Emerson

At the end of every quarter, I challenge my graduate and undergraduate students to reflect upon how their artistic experiences and perceptions have changed through the course of their observations, lesson planning, and collaborations. I ask them to reflect on the following questions:

- What have you observed about young children's artistic development?
- Why are the performing arts important?
- What opportunities and skills do music, theater, dance, and musical theater foster that are not necessarily present in other academic subjects?

Reflection is an important and necessary part of the teaching profession and a skill that most all teachers are accustomed to practicing. We reflect on our practice daily as we teach a short activity, a lesson, or a unit. We reflect on our relationships with our students, the parents in the school, and our colleagues. We reflect on our professionalism, new concepts, and ideas that can inform our teaching practice.

What is it that the performing arts suggest about our lives? Our society and culture? What do music, theater, dance, and musical theater afford us and our students? As you continue to find a place for the performing arts in your classroom, here are some ideas for continuing the cycle of artistic reflection that is central to this book and to building your philosophy of integrating the performing arts:

Keep an Artistic Journal—Going beyond the teaching journals that many educators faithfully reflect within, create a collection of writing about your artistic experiences. Document your engagement with music, theater, dance, and musical theater. Did you see a new show? Listen to a new band? How did these experiences impact you? How did you feel?

Become an Artistic Anthropologist—In a naturalistic setting (such as a playground, toy store, or park), observe a young child engaging in play. Notice whether the child is alone or with family or friends. Document whether there is a catalyst for any artistic behaviors or interactions (such as props or music), and note the child's artistic behaviors. Focus on what is observable (such as tapping, kicking, singing, twirling, rocking, stomping), and reflect on what makes the behavior artistic. Consider how these behaviors may inform your understanding of your students' artistic development.

Build Your Musical Repertoire—Start with the music that is most important to you. What are some songs you listen to when happy, angry, or sad? What are some pieces of music, favorite performers, or compilations that have a consistent place in your classroom? Find pieces that are diverse—reflective of various cultures, instruments, and sounds—to share with students.

Find Your Students' Musical Preferences—What are some of your students' favorite pieces of music, and how can these preferences inform the choices you make with your integrated lessons? Ask students if there is a particular, meaningful song or piece of music that they share at home with their families. Find out if there are variations of popular songs. (One of my students once brought a recording of *Jingle Bells* in Swedish!). Give your students some ownership over the music in their classroom.

Go to the Theater—Take the time to see a play or musical in the theater, to experience being in the audience, watching a performance on opening night, or applauding a curtain call. Note any shows that might have themes or content that are relevant to a lesson or unit you are teaching. Get information on school shows, discounted tickets, or free dress rehearsals for your class.

Find Time to Dance—An experience that is both physical and emotional, dancing will help diminish your own inhibitions and make you more open to moving and dancing with your students. It does not matter if it is ballroom dancing lessons or just dancing with your friends and family. Designate some time for yourself to dance.

Create Collaborations—Much of what is discussed in this book reflects the value of finding meaningful teachers, artists, administrators, scholars, and organizations with whom to build collaborations. The strength of the performing arts is in their inherently collaborative nature. Consider how artists work together to compose a song, write a play, choreograph a dance, or perform a musical. Establishing your own partnerships with educators, artists, and families will enable you to create rich, artistic experiences for your students.

Take in a New Culture—Every major city has designated institutions that preserve and highlight the music, theater, and dance that are unique to many different cultures. Find information on a performance of a culture that is different from your own. Visit the center to get information on the performing arts that are unique to this culture. Compare the purpose of the performing arts among cultures to better understand the role music, theater, and dance play within each community.

Define Creativity—Perhaps one of the most challenging concepts to articulate and place within a concrete definition, *creativity* is at the heart of any artistic endeavor, an expected outcome of both the process and product. Through your experiences with the performing arts, find your own definition of creativity, what it means for your students and for yourself as a creative teacher.

Embrace the Performing Arts—An idea that is central to my own educational philosophy, and one that I have stated in many sections of this book, is that *teaching is performing*. The classroom is our stage, the students our audience. Our craft is our art. Embrace music, theater, dance, and musical theater in a way that makes sense to you and your teaching context. Take risks, be brave, and be flexible. You will find that the greatest performance hall is right in front of you, waiting to hear your artistic voice.

References

Bond, K. E. (2001). "I'm not an eagle, I'm a chicken!": Young children's experiences of creative dance. *Early Childhood Connections, 7*(4), 41–51.

Bond, K. E., & Richard, B. (2005). Ladies and gentlemen: What do you see? What do you feel? A story of connected curriculum in a third grade dance education setting. In L. Overby & B. Lepczyck (Eds.), *Dance: Current selected research* (pp. 85–134). New York, NY: AMS.

Burton, J. M., Horowitz, R., & Abeles, H. (2000). Learning in and through the arts: The question of transfer. *Studies in Art Education, 41*(3), 228–257.

Campbell, P. S. (1998). *Songs in their heads: Music and its meaning in children's lives.* New York, NY: Oxford University Press.

Chooi-Theng Lew, J., & Campbell, P. S. (2005). Children's natural and necessary musical play: Global contexts, local applications. *Music Educators Journal, 91*(5), 57–62.

Damasio, A. (1999). *The feeling of what happens.* Cambridge, MA: Harvard University Press.

Davis, J. H. (2007). *Why our schools need the arts.* New York, NY: Teachers College Press.

Eccles, J. S. (1999). The development of children ages 6 to 14. *The Future of Children When School is Out, 9*(2), 30–44.

Eisner, E. W. (1999). Getting down to basics in arts education. *Journal of Aesthetic Education, 33,* 145–159.

Fallin, J. R. (1995). Children's literature as a springboard for music. *Music Educators Journal, 81*(5), 24–27.

Feay-Shaw, S. (2001). The view through the lunchroom window: An ethnography of a fifth-grade musical. *Bulletin of the Council for Research in Music Education, 150,* 37–51.

Fisher, D., & McDonald, J. (2001). The intersection between music and early literacy instruction: Listening to literacy. *Reading Improvement, 38*(3), 106–115.

Freedman, M. C. (1990). Readers theater, an exciting way to motivate reluctant readers. *The New England Reading Association Journal, 26,* 9–12.

Gard, R. E., & Burley, G. S. (1959). *Community theatre: Idea and achievement.* New York, NY: Van Rees Press.

Gard, R. E., Balch, M., & Temkin, P. B. (1968). *Theater in America: Appraisal and challenge.* Madison, WI: Dembar Educational Research Services.

Giguere, M. (2007). *The mind in motion: An examination of children's cognition within the creative dance process.* Unpublished doctoral dissertation, Temple University, Philadelphia, PA.

Hale, C. L. (2006). Primary students' attitudes towards their singing voice and the possible relationship to gender, singing skill and participation in singing activities. *Dissertation Abstracts International, 67*(06), 141A. (UMI 3223373)

Horowitz, R., & Rajan, R. S. (2007). *Musicals in the schools draft report.* Washington, DC: John F. Kennedy Center for the Performing Arts.

Jensen, E. (2001). *Arts with the brain in mind.* Alexandria, VA: Association for Supervision and Curriculum Development.

Kindler, A. (1987). A review of rationales for integrated arts programs. *Studies in Art Education, 29*(1), 52–60.

Kislan, R. (1980). *The musical.* Englewood Cliffs, NJ: Prentice-Hall.

Lazaroff, E. M. (2001). Performance and motivation in dance education. *Education Policy Review, 103,* 23–29.

Marsh, K. (2008). *The musical playground: Global tradition and change in children's songs and games.* New York, NY: Oxford University Press.

Mason, C. Y., Thormann, M. S., & Steedly, K. M. (2004). *How students with disabilities learn in and through the arts: An investigation of educator perceptions.* VSA Arts Affiliate Research Project. Washington, DC: The Kennedy Center.

Millin, S. K., & Rinehart, S. D. (1999). Some of the benefits of readers theater participation for second-grade Title I students. *Reading Research and Instruction, 39,* 71–88.

Mizener, C. P. (1990). Attitudes of children toward singing and choir participation and assessed singing skill. *Journal of Research in Music Education, 41*(3), 233–245.

Modell, A. H. (2003). *Imagination and the meaningful brain.* Cambridge, MA: The MIT Press.

National Association for Music Education (NAFME). (1994). *National standards for arts education.* Lanham, MD: Rowman & Littlefield.

Pica, R. (2009). *Experiences in music and movement: Birth to age 8.* Belmont, CA: Wadsworth.

Pitts, S. E. (2005). *Valuing musical participation.* Farnham, Surrey, UK: Ashgate.

Rajan, R. S. (2009). Set the classroom stage!: Using musical theater to support English language learners. *ACEI Focus on Elementary, 21*(3), 4–8.

Rajan, R. S. (2011). Come dance with me! *ACEI Focus on PreK & K, 24*(1), 1–4.

Rajan, R. S. (in press). *Children's experiences in musical theater.* Lanham, MD: Rowman & Littlefield Education.

Reason, M. (2010). *The young audience: Exploring and enhancing children's experiences of theatre.* Stoke-on-Trent, Staffordshire, UK: Trentham Books.

Roberts, K. J. (2007). *Participation in musical theater as a vehicle for understanding of interdisciplinary work in the arts, improvement in self-concept, and music achievement among fifth-grade students.* Unpublished doctoral dissertation, Northwestern University, Evanston, IL.

Singer, D. G., & Singer, J. L. (1990). *The house of make believe: Children's play and the developing imagination.* Cambridge, MA: Harvard University Press.

Turner, M. E. (1999). Child-centered learning and music programs. *Music Educators Journal, 86,* 30–33.

Upitis, R., & Smithrim, K. (2003). *Learning through the arts national assessment 1999–2002: Final report to the Royal Conservatory of Music.* Kingston, ON: Queens University, Faculty of Education.

Worthy, J., & Prater, K. (2002). "I thought about it all night": Readers theatre for reading fluency and motivation. *The Reading Teacher, 54,* 294–297.

Appendix

National Standards for Music Education

http://artsedge.kennedy-center.org/educators/standards/

http://www.nafme.org/

GRADES K–4

Content Standard 1—Singing, alone and with others, a varied repertoire of music

Achievement Standard (a)—*Students sing independently, on pitch and in rhythm, with appropriate timbre, diction, and posture, and maintain a steady tempo*

Achievement Standard (b)—*Students sing expressively, with appropriate dynamics, phrasing, and interpretation*

Achievement Standard (c)—*Students sing in groups, blending vocal timbres, matching dynamic levels, and responding to the cues of a conductor*

Content Standard 2—Performing on instruments, alone and with others, a varied repertoire of music

Achievement Standard (a)—*Students perform on pitch, in rhythm, with appropriate dynamics and timbre, and maintain a steady tempo*

Achievement Standard (b)—*Students perform expressively a varied repertoire of music representing diverse genres and styles*

Achievement Standard (c)—*Students perform in groups, blending instrumental timbres, matching dynamic levels, and responding to the cues of a conductor*

Content Standard 4—Composing and arranging music within specific guidelines

Achievement Standard (a)—*Students create and arrange music to accompany readings or dramatizations*

Achievement Standard (b)—*Students create and arrange short songs and instrumental pieces within specified guidelines (e.g., a particular style, form, instrumentation, compositional technique)*

Content Standard 6—Listening to, analyzing, and describing music

Achievement Standard (a)—*Students demonstrate perceptual skills by moving, by answering questions about, and by describing aural examples of music of various styles representing diverse cultures*

Achievement Standard (b)—*Students use appropriate terminology in explaining music, music notation, music instruments and voices, and music performances*

Achievement Standard (c)—*Students identify the sounds of a variety of instruments, including many orchestra and band instruments, and instruments from various cultures, as well as children's voices and male and female adult voices*

Content Standard 8—Understanding relationships between music, the other arts, and disciplines outside the arts

Achievement Standard (a)—*Students identify ways in which the principles and subject matter of other disciplines taught in the school are interrelated with those of music (e.g., foreign languages: singing songs in various languages; language arts: using the expressive elements of music in interpretive readings; mathematics: mathematical basis of values of notes, rests, and time signatures; science: vibration of strings, drum heads, or air columns generating sounds used in music; geography: songs associated with various countries or regions)*

Content Standard 9—Understanding music in history and culture

Achievement Standard (a)—*Students identify by genre or style aural examples of music from various historical periods and cultures*

Achievement Standard (b)—*Students describe in simple terms how elements of music are used in music examples from various cultures of the world*

Achievement Standard (c)—*Students identify various uses of music in their daily experiences and describe characteristics that make certain music suitable for each use*

GRADES 5–8
Content Standard 6—Listening to, analyzing, and describing music

Achievement Standard (a)—*Students analyze the uses of elements of music in aural examples representing diverse genres and cultures*

Content Standard 9—Understanding music in history and culture

Achievement Standard (a)—*Students describe distinguishing characteristics of representative music genres and styles from a variety of cultures*

Achievement Standard (b)—*Students classify by genre and style (and, if applicable, by historical period, composer, and title) a varied body of exemplary (that is, high-quality and characteristic) musical works and explain the characteristics that cause each work to be considered exemplary*

National Standards for Theater Education

http://artsedge.kennedy-center.org/educators/standards/

http://www.aate.com

GRADES K–4

Content Standard 1—Script writing by planning and recording improvisations based on personal experience and heritage, imagination, literature, and history

Achievement Standard (a)—*Students improvise dialogue to tell stories, and formalize improvisations by writing or recording the dialogue*

Content Standard 2—Acting by assuming roles and interacting in improvisations

Achievement Standard (a)—*Students imagine and clearly describe characters, their relationships, and their environments*

Achievement Standard (b)—*Students use variations of locomotor and nonlocomotor movement and vocal pitch, tempo, and tone for different characters*

Achievement Standard (c)—*Students assume roles that exhibit concentration and contribute to the action of classroom dramatizations based on personal experience and heritage, imagination, literature, and history*

Content Standard 3—Designing by visualizing and arranging environments for classroom dramatizations

Achievement Standard (a)—*Students visualize environments and construct designs to communicate locale and mood using visual elements (such as space, color, line, shape, texture) and aural aspects using a variety of sound sources*

Achievement Standard (b)—*Students collaborate to establish playing spaces for classroom dramatizations and to select and safely organize available materials that suggest scenery, properties, lighting, sound, costumes, and makeup*

Content Standard 4—Directing by planning classroom dramatizations

Achievement Standard (a)—*Students collaboratively plan and prepare improvisations and demonstrate various ways of staging classroom dramatizations*

Content Standard 5—Researching by finding information to support classroom dramatizations

Achievement Standard (a)—*Students communicate information to peers about people, events, time, and place related to classroom dramatizations*

Content Standard 7—Analyzing and explaining personal preferences and constructing meanings from classroom dramatizations and from theater, film, television, and electronic media productions

Achievement Standard (b)—*Students explain how the wants and needs of characters are similar to and different from their own*

Achievement Standard (c)—*Students articulate emotional responses to and explain personal preferences about the whole as well as the parts of dramatic performances*

GRADES 5–8

Content Standard 1—Script writing by the creation of improvisations and scripted scenes based on personal experience and heritage, imagination, literature, and history

Achievement Standard (a)—*Students individually and in groups, create characters, environments, and actions that create tension and suspense*

Content Standard 2—Acting by developing basic acting skills to portray characters who interact in improvised and scripted scenes

Achievement Standard (a)—*Students demonstrate acting skills (such as sensory recall, concentration, breath control, diction, body alignment, control of isolated body parts) to develop characterizations that suggest artistic choices*

Content Standard 4—Directing by organizing rehearsals for improvised and scripted scenes

Achievement Standard (a)—*Students lead small groups in planning visual and aural elements and in rehearsing improvised and scripted scenes, demonstrating social, group, and consensus skills*

Content Standard 5—Researching by using cultural and historical information to support improvised and scripted scenes

Achievement Standard (a)—*Students apply research from print and non-print sources to script writing, acting, design, and directing choices*

National Standards for Dance Education

http://artsedge.kennedy-center.org/educators/standards/

http://www. www.aahperd.org/nda/

GRADES K–4

Content Standard 1—Identifying and demonstrating movement elements and skills in performing dance

Achievement Standard (a)—*Students accurately demonstrate nonlocomotor/axial movements (such as bend, twist, stretch, swing)*

Achievement Standard (b)—*Students accurately demonstrate eight basic locomotor movements (such as walk, run, hop, jump, leap, gallop, slide, and skip), traveling forward, backward, sideward, diagonally, and turning*

Achievement Standard (c)—*Students create shapes at low, middle, and high levels*

Achievement Standard (d)—*Students demonstrate the ability to define and maintain personal space*

Content Standard 2—Understanding choreographic principles, processes, and structures

Achievement Standard (a)—*Students improvise, create, and perform dances based on their own ideas and concepts from other sources*

Achievement Standard (b)—*Students use improvisation to discover and invent movement and to solve movement problems*

Achievement Standard (c)—*Students demonstrate the ability to work effectively alone and with a partner*

Achievement Standard (d)—*Students demonstrate the following partner skills: copying, leading and following, mirroring*

Content Standard 3—Understanding dance as a way to create and communicate meaning

Achievement Standard (a)—*Students take an active role in a class discussion about interpretations of and reactions to a dance*

Achievement Standard (b)—*Students present their own dances to peers and discuss their meanings with competence and confidence*

Content Standard 4—Applying and demonstrating critical and creative thinking skills in dance

Achievement Standard (a)—*Students explore, discover, and realize multiple solutions to a given movement problem; choose their favorite solution and discuss the reasons for that choice*

Content Standard 5—Demonstrating and understanding dance in various cultures and historical periods

Achievement Standard (a)—*Students accurately answer questions about dance in a particular culture and time period*

Content Standard 7—Making connections between dance and other disciplines

Achievement Standard (a)—*Students create a dance project that reveals understanding of a concept or idea from another discipline (such as pattern in dance and science).*

GRADES 5–8

Content Standard 1—Identifying and demonstrating movement elements and skills in performing dance

Achievement Standard (a)—*Students accurately transfer a spatial pattern from the visual to the kinesthetic*

Achievement Standard (b)—*Students accurately transfer a rhythmic pattern from the aural to the kinesthetic*

Achievement Standard (c)—*Students demonstrate accurate memorization and reproduction of movement sequences*

Content Standard 2—Understanding choreographic principles, processes, and structures

Achievement Standard (a)—*Students successfully demonstrate the structures or forms of AB, ABA, canon, call and response, and narrative*

Achievement Standard (b)—*Students demonstrate the ability to work cooperatively in a small group during the choreographic process*

Achievement Standard (c)—*Students demonstrate the following partner skills in a visually interesting way: creating contrasting and complementary shapes, taking and supporting weight*

Content Standard 3—Understanding dance as a way to create and communicate meaning

Achievement Standard (a)—*Students effectively demonstrate the difference between pantomiming and abstracting a gesture*

Achievement Standard (b)—*Students observe and explain how different accompaniment (such as sound, music, spoken text) can affect the meaning of a dance*

National Standards for Dance Education Reprinted by permission of the National Dance Association (of the American Alliance for Health, Physical Education, Recreation & Dance)

The complete National Standards for Dance Education and Opportunity-to-Learn Standards in Dance Education (1996) may be purchased from: National Dance Association, 1900 Association Drive, Reston, VA 20191-1599; nda@aahperd.org or phone 703-476-3464

National Standards for Early Childhood Education

http://www.naeyc.org/

http://www.naeyc.org/files/naeyc/file/positions/ProfPrep
Standards09.pdf

Standard 1—Promoting Child Development and Learning

1a: Knowing and understanding young children's characteristics and needs

1b: Knowing and understanding the multiple influences on development and learning

1c: Using developmental knowledge to create healthy, respectful, supportive, and challenging learning environments

Standard 2—Building Family and Community Relationships

2a: Knowing about and understanding diverse family and community characteristics

2b: Supporting and engaging families and communities through respectful, reciprocal relationships

2c: Involving families and communities in their children's development and learning

Standard 3—Observing, Documenting, and Assessing to Support Young Children and Families

3a: Understanding the goals, benefits, and uses of assessment

3b: Knowing about and using observation, documentation, and other appropriate assessment tools and approaches

3c: Understanding and practicing responsible assessment to promote positive outcomes for each child

3d: Knowing about assessment partnerships with families and with professional colleagues

Standard 4—Using Developmentally Effective Approaches to Connect with Children and Families

4a: Understanding positive relationships and supportive interactions as the foundation of their work with children

4b: Knowing and understanding effective strategies and tools for early education

4c: Using a broad repertoire of developmentally appropriate teaching/learning approaches

4d: Reflecting on their own practice to promote positive outcomes for each child

Standard 5—Using Content Knowledge to Build Meaningful Curriculum

5a: Understanding content knowledge and resources in academic disciplines

5b: Knowing and using the central concepts, inquiry tools, and structures of content areas or academic disciplines

5c: Using their own knowledge, appropriate early learning standards, and other resources to design, implement, and evaluate meaningful, challenging curricula for each child.

Standard 6—Becoming a Professional

6a: Identifying and involving oneself with the early childhood field

6b: Knowing about and upholding ethical standards and other professional guidelines

6c: Engaging in continuous, collaborative learning to inform practice

6d: Integrating knowledgeable, reflective, and critical perspectives on early education

6e: Engaging in informed advocacy for children and the profession

NAEYC.2009. "NAEYC Standards for Early Childhood Preparation Programs" Position Statement. Washington, DC: Author. http://www.naeyc.org/files/naeyc/file/positions/ProfPrepStandards09.pdf "Adapted and reprinted with full permission from the National Association for the Education of Young Children (NAEYC). Full text of the position statement is available at http://www.naeyc.org/files/naeyc/file/positions/ProfPrepStandards09.pdf

National Standards for Elementary Education

http://www.ncate.org/ProgramStandards/ACEI/ACEIstandards.doc

http://acei.org/

Development, Learning, and Motivation

1.0 Development, Learning, and Motivation—Know, understand, and use the major concepts, principles, theories, and research related to development of children and young adolescents to construct learning opportunities that support individual students' development, acquisition of knowledge, and motivation.

Curriculum

2.1 Reading, writing, and oral language—Demonstrate a high level of competence in use of English language arts, and they know, understand, and use concepts from reading, language and child development, to teach reading, writing, speaking, viewing, listening, and thinking skills and to help students successfully apply their developing skills to many different situations, materials, and ideas.

2.2 Science—Know, understand, and use fundamental concepts of physical, life, and earth/space sciences. Can design and implement age-appropriate inquiry lessons to teach science, to build student understanding for personal and social applications, and to convey the nature of science.

2.3 Mathematics—Know, understand, and use the major concepts and procedures that define number and operations, algebra, geometry, measurement, and data analysis and probability. In doing so they consistently engage problem solving, reasoning and proof, communication, connections, and representation.

2.4 Social studies—Know, understand, and use the major concepts and modes of inquiry from the social studies—the integrated study of history, geography, the social sciences, and other related areas—to promote elementary students' abilities to make informed decisions as citizens of a culturally diverse democratic society and interdependent world.

2.5 The arts—Know, understand, and use—as appropriate to their own understanding and skills—the content, functions, and achievements of the performing arts (dance, music, theater) and the visual arts as primary media for communication, inquiry, and engagement among elementary students.

2.6 Health education—Know, understand, and use the major concepts in the subject matter of health education to create opportunities for student development and practice of skills that contribute to good health.

2.7 Physical education—Know, understand, and use—as appropriate to their own understanding and skills—human movement and physical activity as central elements to foster active, healthy life styles and enhanced quality of life for elementary students.

Instruction

3.1 Integrating and applying knowledge for instruction—Plan and implement instruction based on knowledge of students, learning theory, connections across the curriculum, curricular goals, and community.

3.2 Adaptation to diverse students—Understand how elementary students differ in their development and approaches to learning, and create instructional opportunities that are adapted to diverse students.

3.3 Development of critical thinking and problem solving—Understand and use a variety of teaching strategies that encourage elementary students' development of critical thinking and problem solving.

3.4 Active engagement in learning—Use their knowledge and understanding of individual and group motivation and behavior among students at the K–6 level to foster active engagement in learning, self motivation, and positive social interaction and to create supportive learning environments.

3.5 Communication to foster collaboration—Use their knowledge and understanding of effective verbal, nonverbal, and media communication techniques to foster active inquiry, collaboration, and supportive interaction in the elementary classroom.

Assessment

4.0 Assessment for instruction—Know, understand, and use formal and informal assessment strategies to plan, evaluate and strengthen instruction that will promote continuous intellectual, social, emotional, and physical development of each elementary student.

Professionalism

5.1 Professional growth, reflection, and evaluation—Are aware of and reflect on their practice in light of research on teaching, professional ethics, and resources available for professional learning; they continually evaluate the effects of their professional decisions and actions on students, families and other professionals in the learning community and actively seek out opportunities to grow professionally.

5.2 Collaboration with families, colleagues, and community agencies—Know the importance of establishing and maintaining a positive collaborative relationship with families, school colleagues, and agencies in the larger community to promote the intellectual, social, emotional, physical growth and well-being of children.

Association for Childhood Education International (2007). *Association for Childhood Education International Elementary Education Standards and Supporting Explanation*, available at http://acei.org/

Common Core State Standards

http://www.corestandards.org/the-standards

Math Standards

Kindergarten

Measurement & Data—Classify objects and count the number of objects in each category.

K.MD.3. *Classify objects into given categories; count the numbers of objects in each category and sort the categories by count.*

Geometry—Identify and describe shapes (squares, circles, triangles, rectangles, hexagons, cubes, cones, cylinders, and spheres).

K.G.2. *Correctly name shapes regardless of their orientations or overall size.*

First Grade

Number & Operations in Base Ten—Extend the counting sequence.

1.NBT.1. *Count to 120, starting at any number less than 120. In this range, read and write numerals and represent a number of objects with a written numeral.*

Measurement & Data—Represent and interpret data.

1.MD.4. *Organize, represent, and interpret data with up to three categories; ask and answer questions about the total number of data points, how many in each category, and how many more or less are in one category than in another.*

Second Grade

Measurement & Data—Measure and estimate lengths in standard units.

2.MD.1. *Measure the length of an object by selecting and using appropriate tools such as rulers, yardsticks, meter sticks, and measuring tapes.*

2.MD.2. *Measure the length of an object twice, using length units of different lengths for the two measurements; describe how the two measurements relate to the size of the unit chosen.*

2.MD.3. *Estimate lengths using units of inches, feet, centimeters, and meters.*

Third Grade

Geometry—Reason with shapes and their attributes.

3.G.1. *Understand that shapes in different categories (e.g., rhombuses, rectangles, and others) may share attributes (e.g., having four sides), and that the shared attributes can define a larger category (e.g., quadrilaterals). Recognize rhombuses, rectangles, and squares as examples of quadrilaterals, and draw examples of quadrilaterals that do not belong to any of these subcategories.*

Fourth Grade

Operations & Algebraic Thinking—Generate and analyze patterns.

4.OA.5. *Generate a number or shape pattern that follows a given rule. Identify apparent features of the pattern that were not explicit in the rule itself.*

Measurement & Data—Solve problems involving measurement and conversion of measurements from a larger unit to a smaller unit.

4.MD.1. *Know relative sizes of measurement units within one system of units including km, m, cm; kg, g; lb, oz.; l, ml; hr, min, sec.*

Geometry—Draw and identify lines and angles, and classify shapes by properties of their lines and angles.

4.G.1. *Draw points, lines, line segments, rays, angles (right, acute, obtuse), and perpendicular and parallel lines. Identify these in two-dimensional figures.*

4.G.2. *Classify two-dimensional figures based on the presence or absence of parallel or perpendicular lines, or the presence or absence of angles of a specified size. Recognize right triangles as a category, and identify right triangles.*

Fifth Grade

Operations & Algebraic Thinking—Analyze patterns and relationships.

5.OA.3. *Generate two numerical patterns using two given rules. Identify apparent relationships between corresponding terms.*

Measurement & Data—Convert like measurement units within a given measurement system.

5.MD.1. *Convert among different-sized standard measurement units within a given measurement system (e.g., convert 5 cm to 0.05 m), and use these conversions in solving multi-step, real world problems.*

Language Arts Standards

Kindergarten

Speaking & Listening—Comprehension & Collaboration

SL.K.6. *Speak audibly and express thoughts, feelings, and ideas clearly.*

Language—Conventions of Standard English

L.K.1. *Demonstrate command of the conventions of standard English grammar and usage when writing or speaking.*

Print many upper- and lowercase letters.

L.K.2. *Demonstrate command of the conventions of standard English capitalization, punctuation, and spelling when writing.*

Spell simple words phonetically, drawing on knowledge of sound-letter relationships.

First Grade

Reading: Literature—Key Ideas and Details

RL.1.1. *Ask and answer questions about key details in a text.*

RL.1.3. *Describe characters, settings, and major events in a story, using key details.*

Reading: Informational Text—Craft and Structure

RI.1.4. *Ask and answer questions to help determine or clarify the meaning of words and phrases in a text.*

Speaking & Listening—Comprehension and Collaboration

SL.1.1. *Participate in collaborative conversations with diverse partners about grade 1 topics and texts with peers and adults in small and larger groups.*

Follow agreed-upon rules for discussions (e.g., listening to others with care, speaking one at a time about the topics and texts under discussion).

Build on others' talk in conversations by responding to the comments of others through multiple exchanges.

Second Grade

Reading: Literature—Craft and Structure

RL.2.4. *Describe how words and phrases (e.g., regular beats, alliteration, rhymes, repeated lines) supply rhythm and meaning in a story, poem, or song.*

Reading: Informational Text—Key Ideas and Details

RI.2.3. *Describe the connection between a series of historical events, scientific ideas or concepts, or steps in technical procedures in a text.*

Reading: Informational Text—Craft and Structure

RI.2.4. *Determine the meaning of words and phrases in a text relevant to a grade 2 topic or subject area.*

RI.2.5. *Know and use various text features (e.g., captions, bold print, subheadings, glossaries, indexes, electronic menus, icons) to locate key facts or information in a text efficiently.*

RI.2.6. *Identify the main purpose of a text, including what the author wants to answer, explain, or describe.*

Writing—Research to Build and Present Knowledge

W.2.7. *Participate in shared research and writing projects (e.g., record science observations).*

Speaking & Listening—Presentation of Knowledge and Ideas

SL.2.4. *Tell a story or recount an experience with appropriate facts and relevant, descriptive details, speaking audibly in coherent sentences.*

SL.2.5. *Create [audio] recordings of stories or poems; add drawings or other visual displays to stories or recounts of experiences when appropriate to clarify ideas, thoughts, and feelings.*

Third Grade

Reading: Informational Text—Key Ideas and Details

RI.3.3. *Describe the relationship between a series of historical events, scientific ideas or concepts, or steps in technical procedures in a text, using language that pertains to time, sequence, and cause/effect.*

Reading: Foundational Skills—Phonics and Word Recognition

RF.3.3. *Know and apply grade-level phonics and word analysis skills in decoding words.*

Identify and know the meaning of the most common prefixes and derivational suffixes.

Decode words with common Latin suffixes.

Decode multisyllable words.

Read grade-appropriate irregularly spelled words.

Writing—Text Types and Purposes

W.3.3. *Write narratives to develop real or imagined experiences or events using effective technique, descriptive details, and clear event sequences.*

Establish a situation and introduce a narrator and/or characters; organize an event sequence that unfolds naturally.

Use dialogue and descriptions of actions, thoughts, and feelings to develop experiences and events or show the response of characters to situations.

Use temporal words and phrases to signal event order.

Provide a sense of closure

Speaking & Listening—Comprehension and Collaboration

SL.3.3. *Ask and answer questions about information from a speaker, offering appropriate elaboration and detail.*

SL.3.4. *Report on a topic or text, tell a story, or recount an experience with appropriate facts and relevant, descriptive details, speaking clearly at an understandable pace.*

Fourth Grade

Reading: Literature—Key Ideas and Details

RL.4.2. *Determine a theme of a story, drama, or poem from details in the text; summarize the text.*

RL.4.3. *Describe in depth a character, setting, or event in a story or drama, drawing on specific details in the text (e.g., a character's thoughts, words, or actions).*

Reading: Literature—Craft and Structure

RL.4.6. *Compare and contrast the point of view from which different stories are narrated, including the difference between first- and third-person narrations.*

Fifth Grade

Reading: Literature—Key Ideas and Details

RL.5.1. *Quote accurately from a text when explaining what the text says explicitly and when drawing inferences from the text.*

RL.5.2. *Determine a theme of a story, drama, or poem from details in the text, including how characters in a story or drama respond to challenges or how the speaker in a poem reflects upon a topic; summarize the text.*

Writing—Text Types and Purposes

W.5.3. *Write narratives to develop real or imagined experiences or events using effective technique, descriptive details, and clear event sequences.*

Orient the reader by establishing a situation and introducing a narrator and/or characters; organize an event sequence that unfolds naturally.

Use narrative techniques, such as dialogue, description, and pacing, to develop experiences and events or show the responses of characters to situations.

Use a variety of transitional words, phrases, and clauses to manage the sequence of events.

Use concrete words and phrases and sensory details to convey experiences and events precisely.

Provide a conclusion that follows from the narrated experiences or events.

Speaking & Listening—Presentation of Knowledge and Ideas

SL.5.4. *Report on a topic or text or present an opinion, sequencing ideas logically and using appropriate facts and relevant, descriptive details to support main ideas or themes; speak clearly at an understandable pace.*

Index

CORWIN

A SAGE Company

The Corwin logo—a raven striding across an open book—represents the union of courage and learning. Corwin is committed to improving education for all learners by publishing books and other professional development resources for those serving the field of PreK–12 education. By providing practical, hands-on materials, Corwin continues to carry out the promise of its motto: **"Helping Educators Do Their Work Better."**